RELIGION INC.
The Church of Scientology

'...falsehood must become
exposed by truth –
and truth, though fought,
always in the end prevails.'

L. RON HUBBARD,
My Philosophy, 1965

RELIGION INC.

The Church of Scientology

Stewart Lamont

LONDON

First published in Great Britain 1986
by HARRAP Ltd
19–23 Ludgate Hill, London EC4M 7PD

ISBN 0 245-54334-1

Printed and bound in Great Britain

Contents

Illustrations

Acknowledgements

It may seem bizarre in the light of the conclusions at which this book arrives, that some of the people I have to thank most for help, information and co-operation in writing it, are officers of the Church of Scientology. My gratitude is nonetheless sincere and although I know that I may be accused of biting the hand that fed me, I should make it clear that it was my purpose to hear all shades of opinion both for and against Scientology with an open mind. After collecting and studying the evidence by interview, from documents and published material, the fact that I felt compelled to make adverse comments upon L. Ron Hubbard and his religion is, I believe, a reflection upon the content of that evidence rather than upon any bias or capricious ingratitude upon my part. I hope it does not sound too patronizing to say that I hope that many of the friendly people within the Church of Scientology (and there are many unaware of the true nature and practices of their church) may one day come to a similar decision when they view the evidence away from the glow of uncritical commitment.

In particular, I would like to thank Mike Garside, the Director of Public Affairs of Scientology in the UK, who, along with his team at Saint Hill in East Grinstead, supplied me with material and allowed me access to Scientology organizations; Rich Haworth, then Director of Public Affairs at Flag HQ in Clearwater, Florida when I visited there in September 1984; Mrs Shirley Young and Mrs Susan Jones, who were my chaperons in Los Angeles; Mr Marshall Goldblatt for generous hospitality, and Rev Heber Jentzsch, President of the Church of Scientology International.

Among the disaffected Scientologists and 'independents' I would particularly like to thank are: John Atack of East Grinstead; Robin Scott and his wife Adrienne at Candacraig, Strathdon; John

McMaster; Neville Chamberlain; 'Alyson'; and Gulliver Smithers. From the opponents of Scientology I would like to single out the Clark family: Dr John Clark MD of Harvard Medical School, his wife Eleanor and daughter Cathy; Dr Michael Langone of the American Family Foundation; and Boston attorney, Michael Flynn.

Other sources of material and assistance were the Editor of the *Sunday Times*, Andrew Neil, and Julian Browne of the Colour Magazine; Kevin Holland of Reader's Digest; Sarah Hogge for permission to use her study undertaken within the Religious Studies Department at Lancaster University; Peter Clarke of the Centre for New Religious Movements at King's College, London; Professor Roy Wallis and Dr Steve Bruce of the Department of Sociology at Queen's University, Belfast.

Last, but most of all, I would like to thank my friend and agent, Andrew Hewson; and Simon Scott, Editorial Director of Harrap, for encouragement, advice and in the journalistic cliché, for 'doing the biz'.

STEWART LAMONT

Prologue

IT WASN'T a bad substitute for paradise: the rolling hills, the mani-cured landscape gardens, stitched into a lush patchwork by the long, straight, freshly painted white fences. The scrub which is a common feature of the hills south of Creston in Southern California had been meticulously cleared from the 160 acre ranch, designed originally for horse training. The quarter-mile track was still there, plus a grand-stand painted white and an observation tower. Wild life abounded and in the hothouse corn stalks grew alongside orchids. The tri-level ranch house sat atop a hill overlooking a lake. A satellite dish and pool were perched beneath a patio and sun porch. The lord of this manor might have been forgiven for thinking he had found heaven on earth.

As the winter sun reached its highest point on Monday, 27 January 1986, two station-wagons turned slowly out of the ranch gates and drove up Donovan Road making for the port of San Luis Obispo, which lay a few miles away on the coast. There a boat was waiting to help the occupants perform their macabre and secret task.

In the front seat of the lead car were two lawyers: Earle Cooley and John Peterson. Cooley was a tall man of vast bulk who had weighed in on the side of the Church of Scientology in several court cases before becoming one of its most influential members. He had once spent a few hours cooling off in the cells for contempt of court when he had defended his clients too zealously. The previous Friday he had dashed the hundred and fifty miles north from Los Angeles as soon as he had heard the news. He had spent the weekend with his assistant, John Peterson, who was driving the station-wagon, seeing that everything went exactly to plan. There had been no autopsy on the deceased. But the sheriff of San Luis Obispo County and the coroner had been satisfied with the death certificates and the fingerprints and blood samples with which they had been furnished. They had managed to arrange a swift cremation that morning for the body. With the ashes scarcely cool, Cooley and Peterson and others were on their way to perform one final task before returning to Los Angeles to announce their secret to the world that very evening.

The small silver urn Cooley held between his knees contained the remains of a giant among men — the man he admired above anybody else who had lived. Behind Cooley and Peterson sat a large man with greying hair, his tinted glasses concealing soft and tearful eyes. Heber Jentzsch was an emotional man. A man with a big heart. As well as his personal grief was his regret that he had never met the man whose remains occupied the urn, yet in the eyes of the world Jentzsch was the man who represented the deceased when he disappeared six years previously. Beside Jentzsch sat his wife Karen, a dark-skinned woman who had known their dead leader. Gossip had it that she had been a night-club hostess before Scientology had given her a new career, one in which she had gone quickly and ruthlessly to the top before her marriage to the President of the Church of Scientology International.

The other station-wagon contained three people: two men and a woman. It drew ahead as they neared the jetty to meet the skipper of the large motor-boat which they had chartered for the morning. The man did not know that this was to be the 'Commodore's' last voyage or that the funeral he was to witness that morning in the gentle calm of a bay in the Pacific Ocean on the Californian coast was that of a man who had started his life's voyage as a Navy man in these very waters and ended it as a notorious recluse. Not for a moment did he suspect that the name of the bulky Caucasian whose ashes occupied the silver urn was Lafayette Ron Hubbard, science-fiction writer and founder of a religion which had millions of followers worldwide. Now only seven of those followers were present, as the sun glinted on the ocean around their small vessel, to say goodbye to Ron as they affectionately and devotedly knew him. There was a reason for the seclusion and the privacy. It was a very simple reason. Those millions of followers around the world did not know that Hubbard was dead. The seven secret mourners intended to keep it that way for at least a few more hours.

The youngest of the seven, a slim youth in his early twenties with a drooping moustache, was dressed in black trousers and a white short-sleeved shirt. The insignia and epaulettes he wore were not from the United States Navy, but the badges of the Sea Organization, the elite corps of Scientology. Commander David Miscavige opened a slim volume bound in maroon leather and began to read, his strong, deep voice trembling with emotion. *'The finely grist mill of time is spent in service such as yours,'* he began. *'We gained from Ron, who gave to us from his past the ability to live and fare against the tides and storms of fate. It's true we've lost his shoulder up against the wheel and lost as well his counsel and his strength. But lost them only for a while.'*

As the blank verse from Scientology's book of ceremonies was read, two mourners stood with their heads bowed, looking into the water. Pat and Annie Broeker were husband and wife and the only two people, apart from Miscavige, who knew where and how Ron Hubbard had lived these past three years. Pat Broeker was well suited to such clandestine activities, He had a voracious appetite for spy stories, fictional and factual, and had the nickname within Scientology of '007'. He was in his mid thirties, a High School graduate who had attended college but had been no high flier. His succession of posts within Scientology had resulted in his being 'busted' from every one except the last, which was as a financial courier to Hubbard himself. That post proved to be providential in 1980 when Hubbard learned that the authorities were about to force him into court. He disappeared and Pat and Annie Broeker became his only link with the outside world.

'We do not tremble faced with death — we know that living is not breath. Prevail! Go, Ron, and take the life that offers now, and live in good expectancy that we will do our part.'

Annie Broeker let a tear glisten on her cheek. She was Pat Broeker's third wife. But in this marriage Annie was the dominant partner. Now in her late twenties, she had fifteen years of service in the Sea Org and despite being 'busted' in 1979 from her post as deputy commanding officer of the organization by Hubbard's wife, Mary Sue, with whom 'bad blood' still existed, she had survived. She was tough. 5' 6" in height, she stood 2" higher than Miscavige and above her husband in the pecking order.

'Your debts are paid. This chapter of thy life is shut. Go now, dear Ron, and live once more in happier time and place. Thank you, Ron. And now here lift up your eyes and say to him goodbye.' David Miscavige was nearing the end of the funeral service written by Ron Hubbard, although seldom performed throughout the hundreds of Scientology churches scattered round the world. For twenty years now Ron had developed the doctrine of its 'religious technology' or 'tech' as he called it. He had administered it through memos and

bulletins from the Hubbard Communications Office. If the tech was Scientology's Bible, the HCOBs were its canon law. Neatly bound in green folders, they defined what to do, how to do it, and to whom to do it. Ron had even covered the present circumstances.

The Press, those 'merchants of chaos', and the Government, stacked full of 'Suppressive Persons', would have a field-day when they realized that Ron had 'dropped the body', Miscavige reflected. They would move in for the kill. It would lead to severe strain on the orgs. Where would the leadership come from? They had always relied on Ron's word to settle policy matters. In recent years outsiders had been told that he had retired to devote himself to study and writing, but insiders knew that Ron was always there in memo or in spirit. Now they would not know where to turn. That was why David Miscavige had to keep his control. As Ron's protégé he had the task of 'keeping the show on the road' and 'getting the stats up'.

'Come, friends, he is all right and he is gone. We have our work to do, and he has his. He will be welcome there.' Miscavige raised his hand in a spontaneous salute to the leader to whom he was devoted. The ocean air was not suited to his asthma. His enemies called him the 'asthmatic dwarf' behind his back. Those who had felt the lash of his tongue usually changed it to 'poison dwarf'.

Despite his youth and his size, Miscavige had a reputation for getting things done. He had learned from Ron that if a little hysterical screaming and shouting was necessary to achieve something, you didn't think twice — you shouted. He had used the technique to great effect at the Mission Holders' Conference in San Francisco in 1982. It had been a tense time. The grasp on power which the founding documents of the Religious Technology Center had granted to him and his colleagues was incomplete until he was seen to be in control. The next task had been to remove those who might challenge that authority. Ron could not help him. He had been incapacitated by a severe stroke, far worse than the one he had suffered in 1975. As Ron lay dying, David Miscavige knew that the Religious Technology Center was the only thing that could save Scientology. It protected him from prosecution, it safeguarded the tech and the orgs and it gave him the authority he needed to get the job done. The body had been properly certified and all formalities had been completed. The 'high crime' would have been to stand by and watch the enemies of Scientology destroy the organization that had nurtured him since he was a small child. He was not ashamed to look on Ron as a father figure. To his enemies Scientology was a cult, a con, a corporation marketing false religion. To David Miscavige, it was all he knew.

What you have just read is mostly fictional. However, the characters are real. There *is* a ranch at San Luis Obispo in Southern California. L. Ron Hubbard mysteriously disappeared in 1980. The Religious Technology Center *does* own the Scientology trademarks which bring in millions of dollars per month worldwide. David Miscavige, a relatively inexperienced member of the full-time staff of the Church of Scientology, became within months its most influential figure. All that is documented and acknowledged. But six years after he disappeared and became a recluse, it was still not known whether Ron Hubbard was alive or dead.

Then on Monday night, 27 January 1986, Earle Cooley, Chief Counsel for the Church of Scientology, and Heber Jentzsch, President of the Church of Scientology International, made their fateful announcement. Hubbard was 'officially' dead. They explained that he had left the bulk of his multi-million dollar estate to the Church of Scientology. They revealed that his body had been cremated and its ashes scattered. No post mortem had been carried out, and although the coroner of San Luis Obispo County had received blood specimens and fingerprints, speculation inevitably arose that Hubbard did not die in January 1986 but had been dead for over two years. During the past six years since he had disappeared immense changes had taken place in the leadership of the organization he founded. During that time his followers were encouraged to believe that he was still keeping a watchful eye on matters from his secret retreat, now revealed to have been a ranch near San Luis Obispo, 150 miles north west of Los Angeles. His followers continued to act as if he were still alive. He was away studying for another book, they said. He was entitled to his privacy, they argued, when asked why he did not come out of seclusion to answer the charges made against him. He was no longer in charge of Scientology, they protested, and could not be brought to court to justify some of the malpractices of those who were.

His opponents took a different view. He was in hiding to avoid his crimes of tax avoidance, criminal conspiracy and fraud, they alleged. Far from his having retired from running Scientology, they produced documents which linked him to the burglary by his wife and nine others of Federal offices in 1977. He was laughing all the way to the bank, they said, as money continued to pour into the Scientology coffers in the early eighties. The banks were in Luxembourg and Switzerland.

There were others within Scientology who never lost their admiration for Hubbard. But in his absence several catastrophes befell the organization. His wife and her ten fellow conspirators were imprisoned. A cleansing of the Guardians' Office followed in which the Church of Scientology was forced to admit that many criminal acts had been done in its name. There was a purge. However, the new leaders — Miscavige prominent among them — were resented. Longstanding Scientologists with a string of qualifications from the church were 'busted' from their posts and they left to form an independent movement, but retained their devotion to the 'tech' (the doctrine and practices of Scientology) and their personal loyalty to Hubbard. They were declared 'Suppressive Persons' by the church. 'Declares' (effectively ex-communication orders imposing a ban on associating with their former friends within the official church) began to pour forth. A bitter battle ensued with both movements fighting to win converts, the official church from outside its own ranks, and thus to bring fresh money into the rapidly emptying coffers. The independents lowered their prices for courses in Scientology and were accused by the official church of 'squirrelling the tech' — as great a crime in their eyes as heresy was to medieval theologians. If the penalty stopped somewhat short of that advocated by Aquinas for counterfeiters of the faith, the animosity was no less than that which the Inquisition felt for its victims. The church which had campaigned so virulently against psychiatrists and governments for 'persecuting' it, found itself conducting a crusade against its own adherents.

One result of this was that disaffected Scientologists began to campaign against the cult. They duplicated memos, disclosed confidential processes, vilified the official church and joined in lawsuits as prosecution witnesses. What emerged was a mountain of testimony, much of it unfavourable to Scientology. Journalists seized on these revelations but until now the inside information has not been collected and published in book form.

Another consequence was that the Church of Scientology realized that it had either to reform its ways or be subject to wholesale attack in the courts and in the media. I have benefited from this more open policy in that I have had the co-operation of the Church of Scientology in writing this book. I have also had the advantage of talking at length to dissident Scientologists, former members of the church who now repudiate it utterly, and the two men whom Scientology regards as its public enemies numbers one and two: Boston attorney Michael Flynn and Harvard psychiatrist Dr John Clark.

Faced with friendliness and co-operation from all these irreconcilable sources, my task was made more difficult, not easier. I originally wanted to write a book telling the story without offending anyone, but the more written material and personal evidence I gathered, the more I became convinced that despite my good intentions and those of many Scientologists, I could not avoid the verdict that Scientology does more harm than good and that its founder Ron Hubbard was more of an evil genius than an idol with feet of clay.

1 L. Ron Hubbard: Guru, God or Demon?

IT WAS Mr Justice Latey in the Royal Courts of Justice on 23 July 1984 who made the most swingeing public attack on L. Ron Hubbard's credibility yet mounted. He was trying a custody case involving a ten-year-old boy and an eight-year-old girl. Their mother had left Scientology and contended that if the children remained with their father they would be brought up as Scientologists and severely damaged. The teachings and practices of Scientology became an issue in the trial, as did the character and conduct of its founder, Lafayette Ron Hubbard. Mr Justice Latey described Hubbard variously in the course of his judgement as a 'charlatan and worse'; 'a cynical liar'; 'grimly reminiscent of Hitler'; and his church as 'corrupt, sinister and dangerous'. On the other hand, Hubbard's followers saw him as a unique spiritual teacher who had an insight into the mysteries of life, a guru who had been a prolific science-fiction writer (with claims of over twenty-three million books sold) and teacher, pouring forth articles, memoranda and books on the subject of Dianetics, which he transformed into the religion of Scientology.

Where there is such a sharp divergence over a person it is usual to turn to the published facts as any historian would. This is where Hubbard achieves a unique distinction among controversial figures. Not even the facts about him are beyond dispute. That he was born on 13 March 1911 in Tilden, Nebraska, is about the only agreed fact. Thereafter the claims Hubbard made for himself in submitting material to reference works (or the claims that were made on his behalf by his zealous admirers) part company with the facts. Even a little detail such as the claim that he grew up on a ranch owned by his grandparents in Montana is completely untrue. His exploits as an explorer or as a young boy travelling extensively in the Far East, sitting at the feet of gurus, are as fictional as any of his later sci-fi stories. The picture of a romantic adventurer invented by Hubbard for himself is forgiveable in a teller of stories as a harmless vanity, but when his academic record is claimed as some kind of authority for his views, or his war record touted as evidence of his courage and moral integrity, and then both are shown to be a tissue of lies, then one begins to suspect that Hubbard was more of a pathological liar than a dreamer. The 'doctorate' from Sequoia University is nothing more than a $20 mail order effort. The nuclear physics course ('the first of its kind ever') that he attended while gaining his civil engineering degree at George Washington University was one of the courses he registered for while there for ONE term — and he failed it, gaining an overall grade of 'D'. The exploits of Hubbard as an explorer and pioneer of geological surveys of Puerto Rico are fictitious. His career as a 'Barnstormer' pilot before the war must have been severely handicapped by the fact that he never possessed a licence to fly powered aircraft, only a glider licence.

All these claims and more have been subjected to extensive research — none more so than Hubbard's war record in the US Navy. He claimed to be a much-decorated war hero who commanded a corvette and during hostilities was crippled and wounded. The only true fact is that he was in the Navy. The rest is pure fiction.

It was the discovery that Hubbard's war record was bogus which sparked off the defection of researcher Gerry Armstrong from Scientology. He had been assigned to assist writer Omar Garrison in preparing a biography of Hubbard and kept some of the documents as proof to protect himself. It was in the court case to win them back in 1984 that Scientology scored its biggest own goal. The case was presided over by Judge Paul Breckenridge in California Superior Court (Los Angeles County) and was brought by Hubbard's wife, Mary Sue.

At first it looked as if the defence documents tracing Hubbard's naval career were to prove damning. When Hubbard was briefly in command of an escort vessel USS PC-815 in the spring of 1943, he ordered its guns to be fired on an uninhabited island in neutral territorial waters off Mexico. He was summoned to a court martial and removed from command. In 1945 he was hospitalized — not from war wounds, but on psychiatric grounds. Documents testifying to his unfitness for command were introduced. Then the Scientologists brought out their star witness, Captain Thomas Moulton, who testified that he had known Hubbard at submarine school in 1942.

Unfortunately for the plaintiffs, under cross-examination Captain Moulton related that Hubbard had told him how he was involved in the first action in the Second World War at Pearl Harbour and how his destroyer had gone down with all hands save himself. Hit in the kidneys, Hubbard had crawled ashore and subsequently sailed to Australia. Captain Moulton's testimony not only stressed his credulity but exposed yet another well-spring in the abundantly irrigated fields which had been sown with Hubbard's lies.

The difficulty Hubbard had in urinating at the time he knew Moulton was not the result of a war wound. Documents in Hubbard's handwriting produced in court showed he had contracted gonorrhoea after sex with a lady named Fern.

In the British case, Justice Latey poured scorn on another claim that Hubbard was sent by US Naval Intelligence to break up a black magic ring in California: 'He was not. He was himself a member of that occult group and practised ritual sexual magic in it.'

Thus the picture of Hubbard as a romancer and purveyor of flim-flam gives way to a darker portrait of a pathological liar distorting the truth about himself for personal gain. His application for a disability pension for a war wound that never existed was cynically undertaken. Armstrong's attorney Michael Flynn tells of a document which relates how Hubbard declared he was going into the hearing for the pension and 'convince the Feds I'm disabled and then I'm gonna laugh at them'. 'This is the mindset which created Scientology, a man who is making these fraudulent claims about himself,' says Flynn.

It was in 1946 that Hubbard was first involved with Aleister Crowley's black magic movement, the Ordo Templi Orientis (Order of the Oriental Temple). The Church of Scientology claims that Hubbard was working as an undercover policeman for the Los Angeles Police Department when he infiltrated a black-magic ring in Pasadena at that time. It was run by Dr Jack Parsons, a top rocket scientist who was a disciple of Crowley. In this instance the facts are not in dispute: Hubbard ran off to Florida with a lady named Betty in a yacht belonging to Parsons and with $10,000 of his money. Soon afterwards the ring broke up. Hubbard's devotees hold this up as a successful undercover operation, but in the absence of official acknowledgement by the authorities of Hubbard acting as their agent, many may choose to believe that it was a case of one scoundrel ripping off another.

The Church of Scientology was successful in obtaining a retraction by *The Sunday Times* in 1969 and in winning an action in 1971 against the author John Symonds and publishers of *The Great Beast*, a biography of Crowley, which alleged that Hubbard's new religion was derived from black magic. There is no evidence that Hubbard continued his occult practices through the time that he was in charge of the cult in the sixties and seventies, but there is evidence linking him with Crowley's beliefs.

First, there is the *Penthouse* interview of June 1983 with Hubbard's son Ronald (nicknamed 'Nibs'), who broke with him in 1959. There are some grounds for doubting Hubbard Jr. as a reliable witness. As we shall see in a later chapter, he has at different times retracted some of his allegations against his father, but in this interview he stated: 'When Crowley died in 1954, my father thought he should wear the cloak of the beast and become the most powerful being in the universe . . . What a lot of people don't realize is that Scientology is black magic . . . spread out over a long time period. To perform black magic generally takes a few hours or, at most, a few weeks, but in Scientology it's stretched out over a lifetime and so you don't see it. Black magic is the inner core of Scientology — and is probably the only part of Scientology that really works.'

The fact that Nibs Hubbard (or Ronald DeWolf as he is now known) still conducts courses in techniques derived from Scientology, for fees, perhaps undermines the credibility of these allegations. His analysis of the dependency of Scientology on black magic is perhaps tinged by his deep animosity towards his father. But the 'mindset' of an occultist, who uses ritual to acquire power and dominance over others, is totally consistent with Hubbard's psychological profile. In his Philadelphia lectures in 1952 he makes the link himself in his own words: 'The magical cults of the 8th–12th centuries in the Middle East were fascinating; the only modern work that has anything to do with them is a trifle wild in spots but is a fascinating work in itself, and that's written by Aleister Crowley — the late Aleister Crowley — my very good friend . . . Crowley exhumed a lot of the data from these old magic cults and he handles cause and effect quite a bit. Cause and effect is handled according to a ritual. . . . Now a magician — getting back to cause and effect and Aleister's work — a magician postulates what his goal will be before he starts to accomplish what he is doing.'[1]

Ron Hubbard was never openly a magician but in cause and effect through Scientology he created rituals and held millions spellbound through the power of his will. How he came to discover the means to

---

[1] (PDC Lecture 18)

do it is a fascinating story. Like Mae West's 'Come up and see me sometime', or Bogart's 'Play it again, Sam', or Cagney's 'You dirty rat', the saying attributed to Hubbard regarding the profit to be made out of starting a new religion, was probably never made by him. Scientologists have drawn attention to a letter of Eric Blair (George Orwell: *Collected Essays*, Vol. 1, p. 304) which ironically suggests that the way to make a million is to start a new religion. Hubbard certainly achieved that, but before the chicken of Scientology came the egg of Dianetics.

Dianetics means literally 'through the mind', although Hubbard defined it as 'through the soul': Since he did not complete even a fictitious course in Greek, the mistake is perhaps understandable. The bible of Dianetics is his book *Dianetics: the Modern Science of Mental Health* (DMSMH), published in 1950. This date has been adopted by the Church of Scientology as the *fons et origo* of its religion and you will sometimes see red-letter events designated 'A.D. 25', which means 1985 or 'after Dianetics 25', not *anno Domini*.[1]

It is uncertain how much of Dianetics was actually discovered by Hubbard. In the late forties he was writing science-fiction stories and spent some time in California as a screenwriter. Whether or not he plagiarized the ideas in DMSMH became irrelevant after its publication, when he became widely acknowledged as the authority on the subject. It defines the principal driving force in life as the will to survive. This expresses itself through eight dynamics — the original four being: through self-preservation; through procreation; through family or race; through all mankind. Thus if you hear a Scientologist saying that someone is '2–D out–ethics' he means that they have been guilty of a sexual misdemeanour or unethical behaviour in the second dynamic. This org-speak is a feature of Scientology in which all terms are defined strictly and processes given technical names by Ron. Like the Red Queen, a word means what Ron says it means. Dianetics postulates the analytical mind which sets men apart from the animals and the 'reactive mind' which absorbs all experiences of pain and pleasure as individuals pass along the 'time–track' of life. Hubbard took an Eastern view that this time–track was cyclic through successive reincarnations. In the early years of Dianetics there were practitioners who violently disagreed with this. It led to some of the first splits within the Dianetics movement.

---

[1] The first Church of Scientology org was opened in Los Angeles in 1954; the Founding Church of Scientology in Washington, DC in 1955.

The theory of Dianetics was developed by Hubbard through lectures and publications. Other dynamics were added. Number five dealt with the urge to survive as a life organism. Six was the urge to survive as part of the physical universe of MEST, which stood for Matter–Energy–Space–Time. Seven was the survival of the spirit or 'theta', as he called it. Thetans are spiritual beings who have realized their potential and are not held back by the handicap of 'engrams'. Up to this state a person is a 'preclear'. Engram-free, they become 'Clear' — a state akin to salvation, but different from the religious concept in that Clears could supposedly be made and measured. The controversial claim was made that Clears recovered from illness more quickly and suffered disease less often, a result which has, not surprisingly, never been borne out in proper scientific research. The eighth dynamic was survival as part of the supreme being, Scientology's nirvana.

Two other dogmas are worth noting. First, the ARC triangle, which stands for Affinity–Reality–Communication. These are mutually related so that if communication is low then it follows that affinity and reality will be low. Secondly, there is the tone-scale invented by Hubbard, which ranges from 0.0 (dead), through grief at 0.5, sympathy at 0.9 and covert hostility at 1.1, to the ceiling of 4.0, which equals enthusiasm. Walking tall at 4.0, the individual would be a MEST clear, free from psychosomatic ills and nearly immune to bacteria. Hubbard extended his observations to declare that some political ideologies were higher on the tone-scale than others. Liberalism has a 'higher tone' than Fascism, which is superior to Communism.

The preclear who cannot recall incidents in his present life while conscious, awake and 'in present time' (known as straight-wire processing), is badgered time and again with the same question until he remembers. Or various techniques can be used by the auditor, the person who is conducting the session with the preclear (often abbreviated to pc). For example: 'The auditor asks the pc to run through a moment of sexual pleasure and then when his pc, who does not have to recount this moment aloud, appears to have settled into that moment, the auditor demands that the pc goes immediately to conception. The pc will normally do so . . .' (*Science of Survival* II, p. 173). Persistent cross-examination by the auditor can break down the resistance of the pc to confronting certain painful incidents or engrams in his or her past. The induction of Dianetic reverie heightens this quasi-influence of the auditor over the pc, but clearly in the right hands Dianetics

23

could be an effective form of releasing mental blocks and trauma. It was a tool that Hubbard was to develop into a complex system dominated by his strong and ugly personality, which has more than once been called paranoid and schizophrenic.

With the publication of DMSMH in 1950, Hubbard had been lucky enough to acquire two influential figures to join the Board of Directors of the Hubbard Dianetic Research Foundation, which he set up in 1950. One was John W. Campbell, the editor of *Astounding Science Fiction*, to which Hubbard had contributed an article on Dianetics in 1948. The other was a medical man, Dr Joseph Winter. When the initial interest waned and cash-flow to the Foundation became a problem, Don Purcell of Wichita, Kansas, stepped in to provide a cash injection in 1951. Purcell became President of the Foundation, with Hubbard as Chairman and Vice-President, and the Foundation was relocated in Wichita. However, in 1952 the Foundation went bankrupt and Hubbard sold his stock to Purcell along with all the copyrights, including DMSMH.

There were many reasons for the fragmentation. The various scattered field groups jealously guarded their independence and did not acknowledge Hubbard as chief. His authoritarian style was a problem and this led to a split with John Campbell. Hubbard's espousal of occultism and his identification of 'past lives' as the source of many engrams did not please those, including Dr Winter, who wanted to see Dianetics accepted by the scientific community. It had been lumped together with psycho-analysis and hypnotism because of its stress on childhood trauma and its use of Dianetic 'reverie'. The battle was fierce, each group having its own journal (*Dianews*, *Dianotes*, etc), and several breakaway methodologies based on Dianetics were formed at this time, including Synergetics.

Hubbard was faced with a problem in the early days of the HDRF. So far the state of 'Clear' had been much touted but there appeared to be no means of agreeing that Clears had been achieved. With characteristic initiative, Hubbard announced that his second wife, Sara Northrup, was one, but when she divorced him, making bitter accusations against him, the status of Clears and of the HDRFs suffered another blow.

Roy Wallis, the sociologist who catalogued the rise of Scientology from its origins in Dianetics in his book *The Road to Total Freedom* (1976), accounts for the popularity of Dianetics in 1950 as a reason for its demise. Like the concept of a 'flying saucer' current at the time, 'Clear' became a Rorschach blot concept which could be all things to all people. They could impose their aspirations upon it. Simply by reading DMSMH they could start auditing one another and, unlike other psychotherapies, it did not insist on professional training or standards for its practitioners, whose claims about their competence could not be verified. In *Marginal Medicine* (1976) Wallis argues that when Hubbard came to found Scientology, he profited from these lessons. 'Scientology was organized from the outset in a highly centralized and authoritarian fashion and was practised on a professional basis. Its theory and method were only gradually revealed to those who displayed commitment to Hubbard and practised its techniques in a pure and unalloyed fashion. A rigorous method of social control emerged and it was made clear to all followers that Hubbard was the sole source of new knowledge and of interpretation of existing knowledge.'

However, in 1952 the phoenix had yet to arise from the ashes of the HDRF in Wichita. Hubbard took himself off literally to the town of Phoenix, Arizona, and opened a centre there in March 1952. He travelled in September of that year to England to lecture in London and returned again in January to find interest in his theories increasing. In between these visits he delivered the famous Philadelphia Doctorate Lectures (1–19 December 1952). These are still for sale on cassette by the Church of Scientology at over $2000 for the set and include Hubbard's notorious reference to the R2–45 process for exteriorisation. In plain language, it means that someone can be released from their body by shooting them with a Colt '45, which Ron proceeded to demonstrate by firing a revolver into the floor of the podium.

Hubbard then 'invented' the term Scientology. Whether or not he borrowed the term is immaterial. He has made it all his own, one of the few achievements which is undisputed. He defined it as 'the science of knowing how to know' and differentiated it from Dianetics, which he explained as derived from through *(dia)* the soul *(nous)*. 'Dianetics addresses the body. Scientology addresses the thetan [spirit] . . . Thus Dianetics is used to knock out and erase illnesses, unwanted sensations, misemotion, somatics, pain, etc. Scientology and its grades are *never* used for such things. Scientology is used to increase spiritual freedom, intelligence, ability, to produce immortality.' (*What is Scientology?*, p. 209)

In Phoenix, Hubbard began HASI (Hubbard Association of Scientologists, which later gained the suffix International) and waged war on Purcell in Wichita, accusing him of profiteering from Dianetics. In late 1954 Purcell switched his support to the splinter group

Synergetics and Hubbard had a lucky break. Anxious to free himself from Hubbard's lawsuits, Purcell gave Hubbard back the copyrights of the Dianetics material. Ron now had the opportunity to have his Scientology cake and to eat Dianetics for breakfast. He took it.

In the next chapter we shall see how the tools of Dianetics became the trappings of a religion. One of the most important of these tools had hardly been used by the Dianetics movement. This was the E-Meter which had been developed by Volney G. Mathison in 1959. Although there is very little that Scientologists do not attribute to the apparently limitless genius of Hubbard, they do agree that Mathison produced the device which with minor modifications has now been renamed the 'Hubbard Electrometer'. Hubbard's original specification was for a device that was capable 'of measuring the rapid shifts in density of a body under the influence of thought and measuring them well enough to give an auditor a deep and marvellous insight into the mind of his preclear'. The instrument which fulfilled these great expectations was a form of galvanometer which operated on the principle of the wheatstone bridge so beloved of school physics labs. It was wired up to two tin cans such as those used to hold baby food or frozen orange juice. The terminals are held, one in each hand, by the preclear and thus measure the conductivity (or conversely the resistance) of the skin of the hands. Obviously this will be affected by pressure, but operators attempt to stabilize the reading for each preclear (the 'body reading') and then look for significant swings in the galvanometer needle. This is also the principle on which the lie detector works and when used to ask a preclear about his 'overts' (wrongdoing), it functions precisely in this manner.

A complex terminology was developed by Hubbard to interpret the readings of the needle. It was a cocktail of slang and pseudo-science: 'theta bop' (steady dance of the needle); 'stage four' (needle goes up an inch or two, sticks, falls to the right and repeats this action); 'rock slam' (needle goes back and forth in jerky fashion); 'floating' (the goal of the auditing session when the needle floats free over a wide area unaffected by questions or commands).

Scientologists usually demonstrate the working of the E-Meter by asking a subject to hold the cans, then pinching him or her on the back of the hand. This will usually cause a deflection of the needle, since it is a painful experience. When the needle has settled, the auditor then asks the subject, 'Recall that pinch'. The needle will then deflect in the same way as in the original pinch, but probably with less intensity. This test is said to demonstrate Hubbard's view of the reactive mind

— that all painful experiences on the time-track are stored until released by auditing. Wallis reviews some of the scientific work done to test this hypothesis. In one test a pc was given sodium pentathol and while he was unconscious a passage from a physics textbook was read and pain administered. Six months of subsequent auditing sessions failed to produce recall by the 'reactive mind' of the incident.

The area of auditing is intensely personal. Two common questions are: 'What are you willing to tell me about?' and 'What are you willing to tell me about it?' Clearly guilt and sensitivity are being looked for by the E-Meter as voraciously as the diviner's rod hunts for water. Persistent questioning will follow 'withholds' (matters about which the pc would rather not give a straight answer). Auditing can thus be seen as a cousin of techniques such as psycho-analysis (where childhood experiences, particularly of sexuality, are tapped) and of psychotherapy. We shall see in a later chapter how this has led to accusations of brain-washing and manipulation, some of which are no more justified against the Scientologists than against any other religion. But in its early days the E-Meter ran into formidable opposition from the medical establishment in the US. It is against the law in the USA to diagnose and treat disease unless as a properly qualified medical practitioner. Dianetics had been attacked from its inception by representatives of the American Medical Association (AMA). Dr Morris Fishbein was widely quoted in 1950 when he called it yet another 'mind-healing cult'.

Omar Garrison catalogues the antagonism towards Scientology by the AMA in his book *The Hidden Story of Scientology* (1974), which is largely sympathetic to the Church of Scientology and is sometimes sold in its bookshops. He contends that the AMA at one point considered planting a spy in Scientology's Founding Church in Washington and that black propaganda was spread by the AMA about Hubbard, particularly that he had received psychiatric treatment. Both these charges are somewhat ironic in that such black propaganda became one of the officially sanctioned tactics of Scientology, and evidence introduced in 1984 in the Armstrong case supports the contention that Hubbard was subject to psychiatric treatment on demobilisation from the Navy. However, it was the E-Meter that gave the authorities their greatest chance in the fifties of acting against Hubbard's organization. Garrison quotes Oliver Field of the AMA's Bureau of Investigation writing to an Ohio scientist opposed to Hubbard: 'We notice in copies of correspondence you enclosed that Dr Milstead of the Food and Drug Administration (FDA) has indicated that an investigation is going forward so far as the device of the E-Meter is concerned and perhaps that activity is the only immediate hope of achieving any interference with the activities of the Scientologists.'

The FDA already had an agent within the Washington church. His reports were eventually to lead to a raid on the church on 4 January 1963 by US marshals, in which Scientology files and E-Meters were seized. The Scientologists were outraged. A protracted legal battle ensued with the Church of Scientology contending that what was involved was not simply an attack on itself as a religious movement but upon the First Amendment to the US Constitution which guarantees freedom of religion. In the course of its submissions it contended that the E-Meter was a religious artefact and if it was held to be an instrument of healing then this would also have to apply to the mass wafers, candles and holy water of Roman Catholicism. What was important here in the development of Scientology into a religion was that if the E-Meter was judged to be a religious artefact then a religion had been created in which spiritual progress could actually be measured and practised without recourse to providential grace from God. It could be assured by performing the correct techniques and by following a manual. It was truly a religious 'technology'. The 'truths' of religion had been rendered as quasi-scientific principles. Salvation was not something which came to those whom God chose, but was open to anyone who paid for an auditing course. That was, of course, blasphemy to orthodox religionists. It was the age-old heresy of gnosticism repackaged in a way to appeal to twentieth-century scientific man. The E-Meter was declared by Hubbard to be more infallible than any pope and was as immutable as any law of thermodynamics. 'It sees all, knows all. It is never wrong.' (*Electro-psychometric Auditing Operator's Manual*, p. 57)

Right from its inception in the fifties the Church of Scientology had established a collision course with orthodox religion and medicine. It also acquired another enemy, the Inland Revenue Service, or IRS. Scientology had been incorporated on 21 July 1955 as a non-profit-making society and corporation. Like other churches in the USA it did not, therefore, have to pay taxes. In 1958 the IRS began to try to alter this state of affairs and to withdraw the tax-exempt status of Scientology. This hostility from Government agencies did much to establish the paranoia about the State which was to lead Scientologists and their founder into many excesses in later years. Despite a growing network of churches throughout the US and a burgeoning income, it also explains why Hubbard sought a new Mecca for his Dianetic dollars in the late fifties which was far from his enemies' influence. He found it in the rural splendour of Sussex, England, in the grandeur of a mansion which was once the domain of the Maharaja of Jaipur.

2 A Religious Technology

SAINT HILL Manor nestles in the woodlands of Sussex, two miles from the town of East Grinstead. A gaudy board advertising Dianetics stands at the entrance gate, and the lodge exhibits a home-made notice proclaiming that its owners have nothing to do with Scientology. So the visitor must pass on through the gates where he will see a large car-park to his left and a notice proclaiming the Church of Scientology accompanied by the eight-pointed crucifix, which, like all the trademarks and utterances of L. Ron Hubbard, has been registered for copyright. Over to the right as the drive continues downhill, the visitor's eye is drawn to a large, one-storey complex built in the distinctive yellow sandstone of the area in the style of a castle. Over a verandah hangs the Reception sign and it is here that students from all over the world get their first glimpse of what was for fifteen years the headquarters of Hubbard's empire: a cramped bookshop (only works by Ron on sale), a tiny old-fashioned manual telephone exchange and everywhere on the walls pictures of Hubbard or posters carrying slogans from his works.

To the rear of the 'castle' is the course-room where students hunch over desks, wearing earphones through which they listen to taped lectures by Ron Hubbard. Open in front of each of them is a dictionary, since a prime dictum is that no student should ever pass a word he or she does not understand. The dictionaries are special Scientology ones and include definitions of certain words which are used in a special way by Hubbard (e.g. 'Having: to be able to touch or permeate or to direct the disposition of'). Presiding at a side table sits the Case Supervisor who assists and tests the students' familiarity with the study material. With its blackboards, posters and tables littered with books and teaching aids, the course-room resembles a schoolroom. Around it are a honeycomb of auditing rooms where auditors and their preclears are closeted in private session. In my several visits over the past few years these have rarely been in use and the students working in the course-room have never numbered more than a couple of dozen.

The 'stats crash' which hit the Church of Scientology in the wake of the expulsions and resignations of 1982–3 has hit Saint Hill harder than most. The castle complex was begun in the boom years when cash and people were pouring through the gates of Saint Hill. It was constructed largely by 'slave labour' and finished only in October 1985. The conscripted workers were members of the Rehabilitation Project Force or RPFers as they are known within Scientology. These are staff members who have gone 'out-ethics' — jargon for sins committed. These might range from incompetence or dishonesty to sexual misdemeanours or uttering opinions subversive to Scientology. Their pay as staff members (usually not much more than bare subsistence level) is halved and they are given low rations while they are working their penance on the RPF.

Within the castle is Ron's room: a study, it was set apart for the 'Commodore' should he ever return. Every Scientology org has one, kitted out with photographs of Ron, a desk and chair, some personal mementoes and a bust in bronze of the man himself. On the desk lies a white Navy cap. Hubbard never saw some of these offices but they were provided for him should he arrive and 'want a place of work'. He did, however, use the large office/shrine in the manor at Saint Hill when he went there in 1959.

To reach the study, the visitor continues his journey down the drive, past the canteen unit, a shabby prefabricated building which resembles a greasy-spoon café inside. The appearance of the hut does not apparently belie the quality of the food. Former students at Saint Hill recall eating low-quality food while paying richly for courses, and in recent years a diet of rice and beans was fed to the troops when income dipped low. Strategically placed around the drive and wooded grounds are loudspeakers and occasionally Ron's voice will literally talk to the trees, booming forth one of his lectures in his distinctive style. Opposite the canteen is the conservatory known as the Pavilion where he really did talk to the plants, which were connected to E-Meters to study their reactions to events around them. Allegedly he produced some giant tomatoes by this method, but like many of the legends of Hubbard prowess, the tomatoes may have grown more in the telling.

The most distinctive room in the manor itself is not Ron's study but the Monkey Room — a large lounge surrounded completely by a mural painted by the artist John Spencer Churchill for a previous owner. In spring 1985 the room was restored by the Scientologist owners to its former glory and I attended the opening at which a bemused Mr Churchill made a polite speech surrounded by Scientologists and the monkeys of every species which had been painted anthropomorphically by the artist with particular personalities in mind. The grim statistics had been put aside for the day and as I sipped my half glass of champagne (perhaps this was to be my version of the RPF), I mused that it was appropriate that the shrine of Scientology, which had specialized in making monkeys out of so many people, should be graced by such a mural.

The religious nature of Scientology is not very evident at Saint Hill. The chapel of this Mecca of the prophet Ron is scarcely used. On one visit I ran my finger along the pews in the chapel, which is no more than an outbuilding of brick bordering the Pavilion. It came up pretty grimy. Although 'ministers' of the Church of Scientology adopt the style 'Reverend' and occasionally wear dog-collars, attendance at services of worship is not obligatory or a regular part of the practice of Scientology. There is a religious service. Craig Mathieson, who runs the UK organization, told me: 'There are hymns and readings from Ron Hubbard and Saint John, stuff like that.' Craig is a Scot whose brother is highly placed in the Los Angeles org and whose 'second dynamic' abilities to attract ladies to his team at Saint Hill earned his apprentices the nickname of 'Craig's harem'. The overseer of the 'tech' for the US is Richard Reiss, an American whose sober manner gives him an air of a divinity don, which is the role he fulfils with regard to the doctrines of Scientology. Hubbard, he explained, is not God, but a spiritual being who discovered a system through which men and women could attain the status of gods (or thetans) through its techniques. When asked where that left the relationship of Scientology to Christianity, Richard Reiss replied with some understatement, 'Jesus Christ does not figure in the religious technology of Ron Hubbard.' That was an honest answer, for, as we shall see, there are several areas of complete incompatibility between Scientology and Christianity, despite the claim made by well-meaning Scientologists that many of their members are both.

The Scientology cross is at first glance a crucifix with splintered ends. The eight points represent the eight life dynamics. There the resemblance ends. Christianity believes in a creator God. Scientology, as we shall see later, believes in a sci-fi cosmology which teaches that the earth was invaded by clusters of 'body-thetans', akin to demons or astral spirits. Not all Scientologists are aware of this teaching until they reach the higher levels, but there is no doubt that this holy grail — of which I have seen a photocopy in Hubbard's handwriting — comes nearer to pagan cosmologies than it does to the myths of Christianity, Judaism, Islam and Buddhism. Why, then, does the Church of Scientology persist with its quasi-Christian costumes, symbols and titles for its 'ministers'? Why does it conduct ceremonies parallel to the christenings, weddings and funerals of Christian churches? The cynical answer might be that thereby it can claim tax-exempt status as a religion. In a Christian culture the 'ministers' can command the status and respectability which accrues to ministers of religion, and attract interest as a moral force for good in the community.

There is no doubt that many Scientology works are of the highest ethical nature. The booklet *The Way to Happiness* is a distillation of the ethical principles of the great religions, and it is a tribute to Hubbard that he could issue something so simple and popular which can be read by the man in the street when many of those religions are struggling to make themselves heard. The goal of 'clearing the planet', the equivalent of bringing in the Kingdom of God on earth (a world 'free of insanity, war and crime'), is altruistic. Many of the campaigns upon which Scientology has embarked are socially beneficial. Its members have campaigned against leubotomy surgery in psychiatry and take a radical approach to mental illness which has come into fashion long after they first espoused it. They work to eliminate drugs through the programme Narconon and there is evidence that many young people have been weaned away from drugs through this therapy. I met Nicky Hopkins, once a session keyboard man with the Rolling Stones, who gave Narconon the credit for his rehabilitation from drugs. In Hollywood a gentle and polite young man named Gary Wallman administered a 'touch assist' (trying to channel mental energy into a sick person by touching him) to me when I had a stomach upset. Afterwards he told me that he had been a 'long-haired, no-good who wanted to kill people'. Now he is a clean-shaven, well-mannered person with a black belt in karate and a job as a lighting electrician on the sets of Hollywood television series like 'Hart to Hart'.

Stories like these cannot be thrown away. But the black belts must be set against the black record of Hubbard. Utilitarianism — the pursuit of the greatest good of the greatest number — is a system of evaluation which does not rate Scientology very highly. One analogy might be that poisonous popes and corrupt cardinals in the medieval church could still not prevent some spiritual luminaries from shining. Another analogy closer to our own time sees Hubbard as a Hitler who gave people a system, albeit an evil one, through which to channel their energies, and while not all the Germans who supported Hitler were evil, so there are benign Scientologists who work through Hubbard's system for a better world.

At Saint Hill Manor in his vast study, Hubbard worked through the sixties improving the way in which his theories were put across. Emphasis was on standardized techniques, which were dubbed the technology. There was no greater sin than adulterating the 'tech' as it was called. This led him to pour forth a succession of memoranda defining processes and terms. These HCOBs (Hubbard Communications Office Bulletins) were epistles added to the gospels of Dianetics and they soon became holy scriptures in themselves. Their style grew increasingly more authoritarian and idiosyncratic.[1] While drug-taking is 'out-ethics' for Scientologists, smoking cigarettes is not. I have never encountered such a high proportion of cigarette smokers among younger people as I have in Scientology. It was suggested to me that this habit mimics the behaviour of Ron, their hero, who was a chain-smoker. It is almost as if nicotine is exempted because of the founder's little weakness for the weed. However, smoking is not allowed while 'in session', i.e. during auditing. Neither is alcohol permitted twenty-four hours prior to a session.

'Auditing,' declares Senior Technical Consultant (UK) Richard Reiss, 'is the heart of Scientology.' It is also the most expensive part. An E-Meter costs over $2,000 and a session of auditing in 1984 was $200 per hour. Scientology defends these prices on two grounds: auditing is cheap compared to alternative services of other 'professionals' such as psychiatry; it is priceless and not obtainable elsewhere. This was one of the sensitive issues when the independent movement began in 1983 and started undercutting the official church's prices.

It is worth saying something about the Church of Scientology's methods of recruiting members. Some recruits come through reading one of Hubbard's books (18%). In recent years strenuous campaigns throughout the world have been undertaken to promote DMSMH in paperback, even selling it on the streets. Its cost is low and it contains

[1] see also pages 40 and 55–6

information about where Dianetics is available at the local branch of the Church of Scientology. However, the Church of Scientology claims that the bulk of its recruits come through a friend or relative (34%) or by word of mouth (23%). Another method is to invite passers-by to undertake a personality test (10%). This consists of filling in a form and answering various questions. Those who have completed it are added to the church's mailing list and invited back to discuss how they can iron out 'one or two problem areas'. This will involve taking a Scientology course, usually the Student Hat (more of which in a moment). This costs a mere $35 and is within the pocket of most people. Pressure will be put on the student if he or she shows interest or competence. Little is said at this point about Scientology doctrines or rules or the authoritarian structure of the organization. Why should it be? It is perfectly reasonable that Scientologists should (a) promote what they believe in; (b) do it a little at a time, without force-feeding their converts. Sometimes opponents of Scientology argue as if its very existence is a crime. That only serves to prove the church's claim that it is suffering persecution. One must be careful to distinguish between the right to believe the earth is flat and the right to charge people large sums of money to jump off the edge.

The potential member is usually invited to undertake more courses. If he has sufficient funds he will be advised that APs (advance payments) will enable him to purchase these courses now and take them tomorrow at today's prices. At this point the enthusiasm of the convert is mingled with vast ignorance. Knowledge only comes a little at a time. You cannot leapfrog up the 'Bridge', the name for the stepladder of courses which Hubbard wrote. You must go one step at a time. Each step costs a great deal of money *(see pages 164–5)*.

The Bridge is basically divided into two sections: (a) personal progress and (b) training as an auditor. Personal progress is aimed first at the goal of 'Clear'. To reach 'Clear', several sub-levels are involved and after Clear the next steps are the OT levels. These are known as 'going OT', which stands for Operating Thetan. This training is only available residentially at a few centres and the costs begin to rise steeply. Pressure is also exercised on the smaller orgs to 'flow them up the Bridge'; in other words, to ensure a steady supply of paying customers for the advanced centres which are at Saint Hill, East Grinstead; Clearwater, Florida; Los Angeles; Copenhagen, Denmark; and Sydney, Australia. There are eight OT levels and some above, which Hubbard is said to have prepared but not 'released'. His habit of expanding the ladder with sub-sections and only issuing one step at a time, or revamping certain courses in the manner of 'new improved' washing powder (as in the 'New Era Dianetics' material reissued in 1978), has guaranteed a steady flow of income over the years. Later we shall look at these OT levels, which are treated as if they were the holy grail itself.

The other branch of the Bridge is to become an auditor. From the basic book auditor who acquires the ability to help others through the application of data contained in books of Dianetics and Scientology, the would-be auditor climbs through a dizzy series of grades until he or she reaches Class XII Auditor, by which time he or she will have joined the permanent staff of Scientology and the Sea Org, a uniformed organization formed by Hubbard aboard his ship in 1967. Its members wear naval insignia and sign billion-year contracts binding them to Scientology in this and future lives. Each step as an auditor has an upper level at which the student acquires the ability to C/S (or case supervise) the level beneath. One of the consequences of the breakaway movement in 1983 was that many of the more qualified auditors were 'busted' from their posts when the Religious Technology Center assumed control, thus creating a dearth of people who could 'deliver the Bridge'.

It is the policy of the Church of Scientology to offer refunds to all those who have made APs and do not wish to proceed up the Bridge. The severity of the 1982-3 purge — which was followed by mass defections — is shown by the figures produced by the law firm of Eberle & Jordan of Glendale, CA for the years 1983-4. Refunds total over $2,064,992, of which $1.5 million was outstanding in June 1984. Not all Scientologists pay the full price of the courses. If they join the staff they receive an allowance per week, free accommodation and are required to work for the church, but in recompense they receive free auditing. However, there is a catch. They must sign a 'freeloader bill', which obliges them if they leave the church at a future date to pay for all the courses they have received at the full rate. Not only has this resulted in freeloader bills of thousands of pounds being presented to former church members, but it clearly can, and has, been used as a means of suppressing dissent and enforcing conformity to church discipline. No one who is in two minds about leaving the only friends and contacts he has had for a decade would do so if he knew that he would immediately be bankrupted by court action the minute he strode out of the gates.

Another way credit is extended to Scientologists is in the form of loans. One such scheme was operated by Lee Lawrence from

38 Morton Road, East Grinstead. His purpose, he says in a letter out-
lining the scheme, is to help Scientologists up the Bridge. 'I make loans
only ABOVE £5,000. I believe that an able Scientologist can manage a
smaller amount without borrowing from me.' The borrower who
signed up with Mr Lawrence would have had to pay interest at the rate
of 30% if he had taken out a loan in June 1982. Although by the
following July Mr Lawrence was offering loans at 25%, it is worth
noting that in the interim the Bank of England lending rate was as low
as 9% (5 November 1982). Lawrence claims that the high interests are
to enable him to cope with service price increases and any losses from
default. However, he has his own scheme to cope with default. 'To
discourage late payments I use a loan agreement which imposes heavy
penalties for ANY late payments, even if only one day late, and I
ascertain that no more than two thirds of the borrower's surplus
income is required to make the monthly payments.' He adds that every
loan agreement is checked and approved by the Church of Scientology
officially. This means that the Church of Scientology cannot argue
that the hardships arising from this scheme are outside its sphere of
responsibility. Two loan agreements which I have examined, dated
June 1982 and June 1983, quote interest rates of 30% and 25% respectively. In the former, penalties of £16 were imposed for late payment
every month for the first year but were 'forgiven' until May 1983,
when they climbed swiftly to a total of £100 alongside the monthly
payment of £155. These sanctions are but one example of the control
mechanisms under which the Scientologist comes should he deviate
from what the church expects of him in behaviour.

Squeezing individual Scientologists for as much as they can pay is
justified by the Church of Scientology on the grounds that recruits are
buying the unique gift of survival through future lives as a thetan.
Giving away all one's possessions would be cheap at the price, runs the
argument. That is indeed what many recruits do end up doing. One
girl I spoke to spent £6,000 in six months on courses which never went
beyond introductory level. She was already a graduate so she was not
stupid and unable to learn the 'tech'. But she had the money, left to her
on the death of her parents. To protect her, because her brother is still
active in Scientology, I shall call her Alyson, but her story is worth
telling in detail because it parallels so many others among the young,
idealistic, middle-class white persons who constitute the typical
recruits to Scientology. Alyson's experiences are in her own words,
drawn from letters and conversations:

'Right now I wonder how I ever got involved, though I must admit to a certain amount of vulnerability at the time due to the death of both my parents in 1979 (I was 26 years old at the time). The money I used on the advice of my older brother Simon, who is a Scientologist, was inherited. I am a diabetic and nearly killed myself on the "Purification Rundown" (mega vitamins, running, sauna, to rid the body of drugs, radiation, etc). I struggled through various courses of auditing, the latter at the reduced rate of £56 per hour because I was a student. I witnessed and was subjected to some terrible incidents. I was pretty disillusioned very soon but they are an extremely clever and strong organization and they don't give up until you've spent every penny you have. I am an intelligent and moral person and have a B.Sc. degree, yet I was duped.

'After a few upsetting and disgraceful incidents I realized that in no way was I going to get value for my money. However, I soon learned that it was not easy to leave ("blow"). It was about six months after I first blew that they finally left me alone. There were endless phone-calls and one staff member arrived on my doorstep and proceeded to verbally abuse me. I returned his abuse and got rid of him but the incident left me shaking with anger and I reported the incident to Tottenham Court Road (the London Scientology HQ) and I received a letter and a phone-call of apology. I wrote to Ron Hubbard twice with a view to retrieving money I had spent (including £800 I had spent on an E-Meter I had never used). I thought of writing to a newspaper to expose them but I was held by fear of retribution, but now the years have passed and I am not afraid any more and would be glad of the opportunity of preventing someone else making the mistake I made.'

That was part of Alyson's letter. She is a quiet and gentle girl. She loves her brother, but Scientology is a big part of his life. 'His wife is anti it, but he loves it, and after he's been to Saint Hill he feels as if he is walking on air. He says that he's had out-of-body experiences and after you go to OT III even if the Bomb is dropped you'll be immune. They only talk about that among themselves because they say the public couldn't handle it if it got out.' Alyson smiled ruefully when she recalled leaving. 'One day I just thought, "Well, it's only money anyway."' But her face darkened as she recalled some of the nastier tactics which were used against her. 'They make you sign overt sheets (that's the things you've done wrong): I was in trouble because I used to smoke cannabis a little, and threaten you if you don't sign that nasty things like accidents can happen. This guy Steve that I knew at Tottenham Court Road, who was really nice, came round once and was very aggressive when I had left and threatened to use the overts against me.'

There are three points worth making at this stage about Alyson's story. In every org there is a sign exhorting Scientologists to 'write to Ron' with the boast 'all mail received by me will be answered by me'. Alyson, like thousands of others, was deafened by silence in reply to her letter to Ron. Secondly, there is the reluctance of the Church of Scientology to implement its refund policy despite the large sum she had been persuaded to put on account. Third, there is the sinister use of overts as blackmail. This is decidedly contrary to church policy but, as we shall see, it has happened and Mary Sue Hubbard admitted in the Armstrong trial that pc folders were used to cull incriminating material against defectors. This is equivalent to using the secrets of the confessional against Catholics and is also expressly forbidden in the codes of Scientology, yet was practised at the highest level by the wife of the founder.

It was at the end of our meeting that Alyson made her most impressive strike against the Church of Scientology. She picked up two red-covered files which represented the records and materials of her £6,000 worth of processing. 'Here,' she said, and handed them to me, 'have them and see for yourself.' I protested that they represented £6,000 and six wasted months to her. 'No,' she said with a smile, 'they're of no use to me.' Alyson may be a sadder young woman after her brush with Scientology but she is a wiser one, knowing what true values are.

It is worth looking at the kind of materials which Alyson was given for her £6,000. Step one is usually the 'Student Hat', which concentrates mainly on study methods. One of the axioms of Hubbard has been much vaunted as an educational tool. This is the rule that a misunderstood word must not be passed until it is properly mastered. In HCOB of 10 March 1965, headed 'Words, Misunderstood Goofs', Hubbard writes: 'There's no hope for it, mate. You'll have to learn real English, not the 600-word basic English of the college kid, in which a few synonyms are substituted for all the big words.' This somewhat startling use of slang in praising the precise use and definition of words, is, like all the HCOBs, framed like a military directive and postscripted with the ever present 'Copyright (c) 1965 by L. Ron Hubbard. All rights reserved'.

These are the three distinguishing features of the materials: (1) the authoritarian tone of the commands; (2) the idea that they are unique and technical/scientific/esoteric; (3) their distinctive style mixing slang with pseudo-technical terms and Scientology neologisms. For example, HCO Policy Letter relating to conduct of auditors, issued on 19 April 1965, states: 'Any staff auditor who runs any process on any org pc that is not given in grade and level HCOBs may be charged by the Tech Sec or D of P with a misdemeanour.' In other words, you do everything according to the book written by Ron and woe betide you if you don't.

This highly controlled system of behaviour is another axiom. Standard Tech delivered in a standard manner is how the Scientologist would describe it. Thus the HCOBs are not insights which Ron offers for development of the person but strict dicta which must be followed. In the 'Guide to Acceptable Behaviour for Students' contained in the HCO Policy Letter of 7 May 1969, there is a commandment to the effect that there shall be no other gods before Ron, viz: 'Do not engage in any rite, ceremony, practice, exercise, medication, diet, food therapy or any similar occult, mystical, religious, naturopathic, homeopathic, chiropractic treatment or any other healing or mental therapy while on course without the express permission of the D of T/Ethics Officer. Do not discuss your case, your auditor, your Supervisors, your classmates, L. Ron Hubbard, ORG personnel or the ORG with anyone. Take up any complaints with your supervisor.'

Other commands forbid sexual promiscuity, especially adultery; or are of the school-rules variety about not dropping cigarette ends in wastepaper baskets. While many are ethically worthy they are presented overall in a manner which reduces the status of the 'student' to that of a schoolboy. Even the method by which concepts are represented by objects or plasticine and moved around a board by the student heightens the process of subjugation of the individual's rational powers. This is even more the case with the TRs (or Training Routines/Regimens).

One of the first of these is 'Confronting'. The student and coach sit facing each other and stare directly into one another's eyes. Any blink, fidget or movement by the student is greeted with a cry of 'Flunk!' by the coach and they go back to the beginning. The idea is to 'train students to confront preclears in the absence of social tricks of conversation and to overcome obsessive compulsions to be "interesting".' The end product, a zombie-like stare, is consonant with the passivity which Scientology demands of its followers towards the tech. A more colourful TR is 'Bullbaiting', which is designed to 'flatten any buttons' (areas which produce a reaction from the student). The coach is joined by others who will variously tease, insult, or shout at, the preclear who must keep a passive countenance. Tickling, making funny faces, absurd suggestions, these are all part of the game and if the pc laughs then the baiters keep on and on until no reaction is produced and the pc's buttons are said to be flattened.

Typical of the routines which are offered to apprentice Scientologists are the CCHs, which stand for Communication, Control and Havingness, which Hubbard developed in Washington in 1957. He wrote: 'The purpose of the CCHs is to bring the pc through incidents and into present time. It is the reversal of "mental" auditing in that it gets the pc's attention exterior to the bank and on present time.' Hubbard adds that the pc must be coaxed as firmly as possible but not too firmly lest he be unwilling to co-operate. But he adds, 'If you have to manhandle a pc, do so. But only to help him get the process flat. If you have to manhandle the pc you've already accumulated ARC breaks and given him losses and driven him out of session.'

The CCHs are a series of robotic commands and actions: CCH 1 consists of the auditor telling the pc, 'Give me that hand' over and over again and replacing it in the pc's lap. CCH 2 is supposed to demonstrate that the pc has control over his body. The auditor commands him: 'You look at that wall. Thank you. You walk to that wall. Thank you. You touch that wall. Thank you. Turn around. Thank you.' Only these words are used and auditors are not meant to enter into dialogue with pcs during session. Pc remarks are met with stone-walling remarks such as 'I'm glad you told me that . . . OK. Is there anything else you want to tell me? . . . Fine. OK', and then the session is simply resumed without further comment. The robotic activity of the auditor cannot fail to have an effect on the pc, especially when CCH processes are repeated over and over again. CCH 3 and CCH 4 are designed to get the pc to mimic movements of the auditor's hands and to mirror movements of a book which the auditor holds and moves around. A further stage requires the pc to move his mind to the wall and in his imagination put one corner next to another. The idea is that the thetan is controlling his environment, not the other way around. Ashtrays and rag dolls are employed and the pc talks to them, giving them commands and moving the objects in response to his commands. For example, I was passing along a corridor in Clearwater, Florida, when I witnessed a man shouting at a chair and manhandling it. 'Don't worry about that,' said my companion. 'He's completing one of our training processes.' Talking to ashtrays goes on for a long time and supposedly reaches the point at which the pc so penetrates the 'reality' with his mind that intention and thought are father to the action itself. Full-grown 'thetans', then, control their surroundings, not the other way round.

A Religious Studies student at Lancaster University named Sarah Hogge undertook the CCH course as a non-Scientologist. The Church of Scientology had previously been wary of writers and journalists taking courses and writing reports. It argues that it is impossible to observe and to submit properly to the training regimen. However, it allowed Sarah to make her study, and her tape-recorded sessions and observations make interesting reading to which both she and the Church of Scientology have allowed me access. We join Sarah Hogge (S.H.) and the auditor (A.) on her introduction to CCHs.

'Whilst on the E-Meter I was asked to define every single word that was used. This included words such as "and", "you" and "that". If I hesitated too long, or got something wrong, the misunderstood word and all possible meanings was read out from the dictionary and I had to define it for each meaning and write sentences using it. The whole process took about two hours and I hated it. It gave me a splitting headache.

'Sessions one and two. During these early sessions I didn't experience strong negative reactions to the auditing. My reactions were more of amazement. I found it difficult to take seriously what was happening. I was being subjected to extremely monotonous processes . . . the auditor with a straight face, and for such a long time. Many thoughts passed through my mind — how the auditor sounded like a robot — how ugly he was close to — how they were trying to "brainwash" me — how much longer would I have to be in the room doing the same thing over and over again. I also kept having uncontrollable fits of laughter at how ridiculous the situation was. The auditing hadn't really started having a deep-down effect on me at this stage. I wasn't yet vulnerable.

    A. You look at that wall.
    S.H. *[uncontrollable laughter]*
    A. OK. What's happened?
    S.H. I just think you're so funny.
    A. Thanks for telling me. We'll carry on. . . . You look at that wall.
    S.H. *[more laughter]*
    A. You look at that wall.

'This illustrates the way in which the individual is suppressed during the sessions. If a comment or question is raised it is acknowledged by the auditor with "OK" or "Thanks for telling me" and the commands begin again. Commands are run virtually all the time. It is not possible to get answers from the auditor about what is happening during a session. (The Church of Scientology would acknowledge that this is correct. Standard Tech means that the exact programme laid down by Hubbard must be followed.) If physical pain or discomfort develops it is not possible to take a break or talk about it. The idea is to carry on with what brought it about in the first place.

    A. Give me that hand.
    S.H. I've got a headache.
    A. OK. Thanks for telling me about it, but the best thing to do is to carry on and you let me know how it goes. Give me that hand.

'CCH 1 was then repeated four times before:

    S.H. I was thinking that it's only the best thing to carry on for you, 'cos I've got the headache and you haven't.
    A. Right. You see, what happens is that in Dianetics and Scientology processes there's a rule that what turns it on turns it off. So if the process has turned this on, then if we just go on, then you should find it will go. Give me that hand.

'CCH 1 was then repeated another six times, CCH 2 four times, then I came out with the source of my headache:

    S.H. That's what gives me a headache. That wall.
    A. Right. Thanks for telling me.

'After going through CCH 2 another ten times the headache went away, only to come back and I was told that I could take only a half-hour break instead of the usual hour. I suddenly became really frightened. I was afraid that any more of these sessions would break me down and that I would become "brain-washed".

    S.H. I want to tell you that I don't find it frustrating any more and that I did before and that it doesn't give me a headache any more. . . .
    A. OK. That's good. Thanks for telling me.'

Sarah was now having disturbed nights of sleep. She asked some of the friendlier students at Saint Hill what the 'cognition' was which she was supposed to experience because if she could reach it, then her sessions would be at an end. Mostly they said, 'Oh yes, we felt like that too. Don't worry, you'll get it. It's really great.' Their laughter from 'the other side of the fence', as Sarah puts it, triggered her next stage of reaction — rage. She became rebellious. In the next session she told her auditor that she wondered what it was like to be in prison. Shortly afterwards he terminated the session.

Sarah became even more antagonistic towards the auditing when she was told that she had to complete this until the desired result was achieved, before she would be allowed to move onto the practical side of the TR course. It was as if she was being forced to take auditing, which she felt was more likely to break down her resistance, before she could get what she wanted. The TRs were the carrot and the auditing the stick.

She was put on an E-Meter, which has often been compared to a lie detector, and asked the question which had been put to her at every session, viz: 'What are your feelings about Scientology?' She said that while there were good points there were also bad ones and that she felt Scientology did not really attract her. From then on, Sarah Hogge was kept waiting for long periods of time. The appointments set up with officials to sort out her 'problem' were not kept. She suspected the bureaucracy was being used against her. Eventually the Ethics Officer told her that she was PTS, a Potential Trouble Source, someone who is hostile to Scientology. She finally left frustrated and confused, realizing that the processes had set up tensions within her that under-mined her objectivity. 'The more sessions I had the more emotional and unbalanced I became . . . I either cried or felt like crying a lot. I felt that I was the victim of something that was beyond my control.'

The Church of Scientology would argue that it is impossible to be audited and simultaneously to observe the process without destroying the effect. This is probably a valid point, but it does not remove the unease which these repetitive drills must cause in anyone who is familiar with methods of mind control. As we shall see in Chapter 6, psychiatrists argue that while auditing is not strictly the same as hyp-nosis and auditors use 'cancellation' statements at the end of a session, the end effect can be very similar. Flattening the 'buttons', constant repetition of apparently meaningless actions, the authoritarian con-text in which the sessions take place, all contribute to this picture. The cycle of emotions through which Sarah Hogge moved is one in which curiosity does not kill the cat but ensures that it eventually ends up eating out of the hand that feeds it. Biting that hand is not tolerated . . . It does not breed zombies but it ensures control. Doubts, dissents, distaste for any part of the 'tech', are firmly and systematically suppressed.

Alyson was recommended to have the Purification Rundown, a

programme which prescribes a diet of vitamins and sauna baths. A glossy booklet (*Purification: An Illustrated Answer to Drugs*, Bridge Publications, 1984) makes the claim that many people have experienced the effects of radiation sickness during the sauna stage and past sunburns have reappeared, only to vanish for ever as they churned their way through the course. However, the booklet insists that the exact prescriptions must be followed and of course these are only available to those who pay for the course (cost £1,284 inc VAT). The Purification Rundown was developed by Hubbard allegedly after studying all the latest literature on vitamins and callisthenics. There is nothing revolutionary about using vitamins, exercise and healthy pursuits to improve health, but it casts doubt on the bona fide of Scientology, whose proclaimed purpose is to help the unhealthy and the addict achieve a better life, that it only spreads such knowledge at a cost. Critics point out that the programme has not been shown to be any more efficacious than simple diet and exercise and its claims are bogus. In some cases (like that of diabetic Alyson), it can lead to actual harm because it makes the patient conform to the system, not the other way round.

There is also the system of 'assists': touch assist; contact assist; and Dianetic assist. These are used on 'somatics' or illness in the body which can be affected by treating the mind. Pain can be diverted by using the touch assist. A finger is placed on the spot where pain is felt and repeated questions: 'Can you feel my finger? Thank you' are made until the pain is lessened. It is an imaginative process. Contact assist means taking the person physically back to the spot where an injury occurred. An electric-shock victim is asked to grasp the spot where he received the shock (current now switched off, of course) and this results in a discharge of the 'engram' which he received from the incident. Dianetic assist is running the person through the incident on an E-Meter. I do not doubt that these psychosomatic processes often result in a placebo effect. In other words, if the patients think they are getting better, they do improve — and I would not wish to quarrel with that. But in the 1974 HCOB on the subject, there are pieces of nonsense such as this: 'There is a balance of the nerve energy on the body of 12 nerve channels going up and down the spine. The type of energy in the body travels at 10ft. a second. The energy from a shock will make a standing wave in the body. The brain is a shock cushion, that is all. It absorbs the shock from large amount of energy. The neuron-synapse is a disconnection.' It is redolent of the quackery and the pseudo-science which gurus perpetrate on gullible followers. One cannot help feeling that Hubbard's megalomania was such that he could not humble himself to accept the advances in science achieved by others more competent than himself. The science-fiction writer had to invent his own system in which he always carried off the Nobel Prize.

By far the most sinister of Scientology exercises are given to those further up the Bridge, who are asked to devise tactics to use in response to enemies of the church. The basic theories and TRs of the 'Student Hat' have been turned into a bond between the individual and the Church of Scientology which demands that they respond to attacks on Scientology with ruthless counter-attacks. The infamous 'Fair Game' doctrine, which declared that enemies of Scientology could be 'tricked, cheated, lied to, sued or destroyed', was but one manifestation of this. Typical of the Church of Scientology's attitude to outside criticism was the HCO Policy Letter of 25 February 1966 which described how to react to attacks on Scientology by feeding counter 'black propaganda' about the attackers to the Press.

There is also the HCO *Manual of Justice* written by Hubbard which outlines procedures to be used in dealing with the media or enemies and includes the spine-chilling phrase: 'There are men dead because they attacked us — for instance, Dr Joe Winter. He simply realized what he did and died. There are men bankrupt because they attacked us . . .' The same booklet outlines the procedure to be followed for the 'entheta' Press who write hostile articles. 'Hire a private detective of a national-type firm to investigate the *writer*, not the magazine, and get any criminal or Communist background the man has. . . . Have your lawyers or solicitors write the magazine threatening a suit. (Hardly ever permit a real suit — they're more of a nuisance to you than they are worth) . . . Use the data you got from the detective at long last to write the author of the article a very tantalizing letter. Don't give him your data . . . Just tell him you know something very interesting about him and wouldn't he like to come in and talk about it. (If he comes ask him to sign a confession of collusion and slander — people at that level often will, just to commit suicide — and publish it in a paid ad in a paper if you get it.) Chances are he won't arrive, but he'll sure shudder into silence.' This version of 'an eye for an eye' written by Hubbard has the distinction of incorporating a malevolent mixture of blackmail and vindictiveness. No wonder that someone from the Church of Scientology has written 'Confidential — for HCO personnel only' on my copy of the manual. It is hardly a work to which a religious organization might normally wish to lay claim.

*　　*　　*

Far from the imposing manor of Saint Hill, in the midst of the Grampian Mountains in Scotland lies an equally, if not more, striking country house set in acres of woodland with walled gardens and extensive lawns stretching out in front of the imposing spired façade of the main building, which is nothing less than a castle in the Scottish baronian style. This is Candacraig House, Strathdon, built and furnished with riches from the Far East. Until recently it was the headquarters of a counter movement within Scientology. Its main purpose was to attract students who would study the upper levels of Scientology outside the church organization. The charges were cheaper and although those running the Advanced Ability Center, as they called it, believed in Hubbard's technology, they had broken with the Church of Scientology. They were 'squirrels' — people who had chosen to follow modified 'tech'.

The moving spirit behind the Center was a businessman in his mid-thirties, Robin Scott, a history graduate of Oxford University who had come across Scientology as an undergraduate and joined the staff of the Church of Scientology in 1973. He met his attractive wife Adrienne in the Sea Organization and they have three vivacious children. But in 1978 he protested about the way some things were being done at Saint Hill. He was summoned for a 'Sec-Check', a compulsory session on an E-Meter to check his 'security' rating. The needle showed 'rock slam' and proved to his interrogators that he was harbouring hostile thoughts. The 'Sec-Check' involves a long list of questions including 'Do you harbour any hostile thoughts towards the Church of Scientology? L. Ron Hubbard? Your org?' A needle reaction on these questions is tantamount to a confession of guilt. Robin Scott was required to sign a confession of his 'crimes'. He became a travel courier and was presented with a 'freeloader bill' of £40,000 for the auditing he had received while a staff member. However, Robin Scott requested a 'Comm Ev' or Committee of Evidence, which is like a court martial conducted by the Church of Scientology to review discipline cases, and he was reinstated. Three years later he left for good and together with his wife was declared a 'Suppressive Person' or one who seeks to damage Scientology.

The Scotts decided that they wanted to fulfil the ideals of Scientology as they still saw them and bought Candacraig. Robin Scott had several business interests and even if Candacraig was only charging a fraction of official Church of Scientology rates he thought that the books would balance. He found, however, that the confession he had made after the Sec-Check was being used against him. This was one of the reasons which had made Adrienne Scott want to leave when she worked in the personnel department at Saint Hill. She had been asked then to go through files which might contain admissions of drug offences, homosexuality or even felonies and to 'get the dirt' on other members of the church. When she refused, she had been labelled a 'non-compliant junior'.

A lawsuit was taken out by the Church of Scientology against Robin Scott in an attempt to shut down Candacraig as an Advanced Ability Center. One factor stopped Candacraig taking off. It lacked the written materials of the highest levels of the OT courses. This was when Robin Scott made what in retrospect he now considers was a big mistake. He resolved along with others to steal them. Knowing that he and his group would be well-known at Saint Hill and instantly recognized as SPs, they planned their coup at a high-ranking Church of Scientology establishment in Europe, in Copenhagen.

Early on the morning of 9 December 1983, Robin Scott picked up Morag Bellmaine and Ron Lawley in East Grinstead and set off for Copenhagen in his Volvo. They drove to the Scientology Advanced Organization for Europe and Africa (designated AOSH EU & AF in the paramilitary terminology of the Church of Scientology) at number 6 Jernbanegade. Lawley and Bellmaine emerged from the car dressed in the Sea Organization Class A uniform, wearing the insignia of senior officials of the Church of Scientology. (They left Robin Scott in the car with its engine running.) They presented themselves as missionaires from the Religious Technology Center (RTC) and told the Copenhagen officials that they had come to check on standards of technical delivery of Scientology counselling at the org. They were given a private room where, upon request, the 'New Era Dianetics for OTs' materials were delivered to them. Morag Bellmaine put these in her handbag and they hurried out of the org and drove off in Robin Scott's Volvo.

Back at Candacraig, in the converted stables block, the Scotts constructed the classrooms which they hoped would become a purified Saint Hill to replace Hubbard's HQ. But in March the following year, the Church of Scientology played a cunning card. A man telephoned Robin Scott saying that he was wealthy and interested in pursuing upper levels of counselling. He was en route through Europe. Could they perhaps meet at Copenhagen airport? Robin Scott agreed. But when his plane touched down on Danish soil, the police, together with the officials from AOSH EU & AF, were waiting. They identified him and he was arrested and taken to the cells accused of theft. It had been a clever set-up and the Danish police had co-operated because theft was involved, although subsequently the Danish court took a different view of the value of the materials which the Church of Scientology had claimed were worth over a quarter of a million dollars. Robin Scott served a short jail sentence of one month and returned, much chastened, to Candacraig.

Candacraig attracted clients who were accommodated in the sumptuous state rooms with four-poster beds installed by the Wallace family from whom Scott bought the house for £110,000. It was more luxurious than the rice-and-beans regime at Saint Hill, but the Scotts were specializing in up-market clientele. Scott continued to run his business in Aberdeen, which specialized in drilling concrete. The locals were suspicious and in August 1984 the Lonach Highlanders, in celebrating one of the colourful festivals of Deeside, gave Candacraig a wide berth, refusing to stop there for a traditional Wallace dram (or toast) because of the Scientology connection. But it was not being misunderstood by the locals which worried Scott most. The flow of clients was diminishing, as was his fervour for the tech of Ron Hubbard. He resolved to sell Candacraig and close down the centre.

When I called in the summer of 1985 the course-rooms were empty and the Scott family were preparing to leave. Robin Scott was by now deeply disillusioned with even the upper-level materials which had caused him so much hassle. He now regarded them as 'mainly fraudulent and harmful'. They were surrounded by hype and mystique within Scientology. They were supposed to contain the secrets of the universe, and to be so explosive that anyone reading them without being properly prepared could die! This shroud of mystery served several purposes. It was a superb marketing gimmick. The OT aspirant felt he was getting something really special. Secondly, the build-up to these revelations created an atmosphere of credulity and conspiratorial secrecy which was a disincentive to anyone who might want to cry that they were simply hokum and that 'Emperor Ron' had no clothes. Third, even if after going OT the students had doubts about the validity of the material, the vows of secrecy ensured that an objective analysis of the material was not possible. Robin Scott decided to lift the veil of secrecy and to go public. 'It is high time the whole fraud perpetrated by Ron Hubbard and the Church of Scientology was more fully and clearly exposed. Although I don't welcome the personal attacks on me that will undoubtedly follow, I consider it well worthwhile if we can get this whole sordid affair out in the public knowledge, so that vulnerable people will no longer be exploited by the vicious and unpleasant monster that Ron Hubbard created with his organization — little wonder he ended up in hiding,' Scott now says.

I was delighted that he chose me to be one of the first to see behind the curtain and felt no sense of impending doom as I descended from my baronial bedroom with its four-poster bed to the study where I was to be shown the infamous OT documents. Indeed, when I read the first page of OT III in Hubbard's own writing, the overwhelming temptation was to giggle.

OT I and OT II are regarded as preparatory actions for OT III (the 'Wall of Fire', a past trauma so horrendous that anyone trying to absorb it without Ron's guiding light would die of pneumonia). Robin Scott calls OT II 'about a hundred pages of gobbeldy gook', so I started with OT III. It reads like science-fiction cosmology. Seventy-five million years ago there was a galactic confederation consisting of seventy-six planets which had an over-population problem. The head of the confederation was named Xenu and he resolved that he would entice the entire population of the confederacy to Earth (called Teegeeach) and blow them up. He did this by popping nuclear bombs into twenty volcanoes and wiped them out. The individual spirits or thetans were thus deprived of their bodies and were collected, frozen in a substance like antifreeze, and packaged in boxes known as clusters. Thus there are billions of disembodied thetans and clusters hanging around earth, too severely shaken up by this incident to control a physical body by themselves, so they cling to life by parasiting on human beings. However, these Body Thetans (BTs) and clusters cause undesirable mental and physical conditions in the human being to which they cling and the route to well-being and happiness lies in removing them. This is achieved by auditing a person back down the 'time-track' to the moment these psychic limpets attached themselves, and then discharging them. This can be a lengthy process and Robin Scott told me of one wealthy man he knew who had worked his way through a million dollars in buying 600 hours of auditing. Contacting the BTs is done telepathically and they are then guided back down the time-track to the moment seventy-five million years ago when Xenu vaporized them, which is known as Incident 2. The principle is the same as in auditing an 'engram' out of a preclear. The auditor commands the person to 'recall that incident' and leads him through it, supposedly discharging the trauma associated with it.

Once through Incident 2 the BT can roam off and pick up a body to resume the karmic cycle of reincarnations like the rest of us. The idea was that the OT and the BT mutually benefited and it was whispered that OTs derived all kinds of psychic powers once they had shaken off the BTs. They could levitate, have out-of-body experiences at will and were free from any manner of ailment, including vulnerability to atomic radiation. I say whisper because when questioned about these claims, Church of Scientology officials will politely tell you that this might have happened to some as a by-product but it is not the aim, nor a necessary by-product, of going OT.

Of course, Incident 2 raises the question of what constituted Incident 1. This is the very beginning of the Universe itself which had been vouchsafed to Ron in a revelation. It, too, created trauma and the reason offered for the lack of total success with BTs was that they needed to be taken further back down the time-track to Incident 1, which is dated four quadrillion years ago. Here in Hubbard's words is Incident 1: 'Loud snap. Waves of light. Chariot comes out, blows horn, comes close. Shattering series of snaps, Cherub fades back (retreats). Blackness dumped on thetan.' This is the creation of the world according to Hubbard, the Big Bang which ended for me not with a whimper but with a giggle that anyone could sit down and buy this sci-fi fantasy for thousands of dollars.

Scott explains the gullibility of intelligent people like himself as being due to success in using the earlier parts of the technology ('wins' or 'gains', as they are known), so that the critical faculty is dimmed as one gets higher up the Bridge. But there were many who were paying through the nose for this counselling and who were not getting 'wins'. They sometimes had to worry about money with which to continue auditing and such worries were not supposed to afflict OTs. Before doubts about OT III and above began to spread, in 1978 Hubbard issued 'New Era Dianetics for OTs' which was like many a brand of washing-powder — the 'new improved' version was launched amid much hype and trumpeting (no cherubs presumably). Like the launch of a commercial product, the effect was to re-stimulate sales. These new levels were known as NOTs and were nothing, admits Robin Scott, 'but a revamped version of OT III'. There were apparently more subtle layers of BTs and of clusters and these new procedures were designed to cope with them. A Solo NOTs level was introduced for several thousand more dollars, which enabled the person to work away at his clusters (with a case supervisor in the background to check whether he ought to be doing more). By 1985 only one person had reached OT VIII.

If the levels up to 'Clear' are easier to understand as a form of psychotherapy rather than as a religion, the OT levels reveal Scientology as a religion with a cosmology, albeit a strange one which sounds like the product of a science-fiction writer, which is, of course, what Ron Hubbard was. But there are other more sinister elements. There is the appeal to the age-old gnostic heresy: i.e. you make spiritual progress by working (or, in the case of the Church of Scientology, buying) your way up a ladder and can look down on those beneath. There is the occultist element. What can BTs and clusters be but demons? Imperfection in the individual is ascribed to the influence of these psychic forces, which then require to be 'exorcized'. This lays the basis of dissociation of personality and occult practices which are the very opposite of religion, which works for a whole, integrated personality. Just as Scientology's doctrines of 'Fair Game' and 'Suppressive Persons' sprang out of the paranoia of Ron Hubbard, so we must look to his schizoid personality for the creation of such a theology.

The top-secret materials have also been the subject of controversy since I got my peep into Creation according to Hubbard. In November 1985, the OT materials were introduced into court as part of a civil case brought by former Church of Scientologist Larry Wollersheim against the church. Although Los Angeles Superior Court Judge Alfred Margolis allowed the evidence, 1,500 Scientologists crammed the court buildings, the Los Angeles Times reported, to ensure that the materials were not subject to public scrutiny. The Scientologists' attorney argued that unsealing the documents 'amounts to the biggest threat to this religion so far'. Although the court resealed the documents after the evidence had been heard, the Los Angeles Times published a similar account to the one I have given (although, perhaps because of differences in reading Hubbard's spidery writing, they call the Confederation ruler Xemu, not Xenu). So far, none of the dire consequences of catching pneumonia have befallen those who were exposed 'illicitly' to the OT materials. I hope after reading this chapter, you will remain just as exempt from the curse.

3 Life on the Ocean Wave

I PUSHED open the door of the decaying block of flats not far from Waterloo Station. The narrow hallway opened onto a room littered with papers and letters and ashtrays filled with cigarette ends. The summer afternoon air was stale and sour and the room was filthy. In the corner stood a single bed with a grubby white quilt. Sitting on it, clutching a large vodka and orange juice, was Scientology's very first 'Clear'.

'This place is just a dump,' said John McMaster. His voice had a theatrical ring about it. His hair was white and his face blotchy around the bright eyes which studied me intently. His hand swept to a chair where he bade me be seated. The man who had once been called 'the magician of the E-Meter' and the first 'Pope of Scientology' by Hubbard himself, is now a frail and emaciated figure. Clutching the vodka and orange, he sipped as he talked, travelling back down the time-track to the days as a young medical student in South Africa when his stepmother first introduced him to Scientology. 'It wasn't a religion then,' he said with some distaste. 'My stepmother used it as a weapon. I told her it was just a tool. That's what it is, a tool.' The tensions grew with his stepmother as John McMaster quit medical school and learned more about how to work the E-Meter. His father reluctantly bought him a one-way ticket to Saint Hill where John excelled as an auditor without ever meeting Hubbard. Then in March 1965 Hubbard offered him a key post.

The next two years were boom ones for Saint Hill. With only six staff in early 1965 and a turnover of £1,490 per week, McMaster helped boost this sevenfold within a year. On St Valentine's Day 1966 Hubbard issued a promulgation that the world's first Scientology 'Clear' had been achieved. McMaster was in Los Angeles at the time and was recalled to Saint Hill to undergo checks to ascertain if he really had passed the test. Hubbard's previous announcements of Dianetics 'Clears' had proved to be somewhat premature and did not stand up to scrutiny. But McMaster passed. On 9 March 1966 Anton James wrote to Hubbard, 'Dear Ron, It's with the greatest joy and happiness that I have to report to you that John McMaster has passed the "Clear" check and no doubt exists that he has erased his bank completely and it's gone. There is no meter reaction at all . . . his presence in the environment brings about a calmness and safety.'

McMaster became a legend among the devoted followers of the 'tech'. The incarnate Clear's speaking style charmed thousands and his touch on the E-Meter brought people like author William Burroughs to be audited by him. Hubbard charged £2,500 for processing, with £50 for fifty hours with McMaster, who was receiving £4 per week. Then he upped it to £250 as McMaster's prowess grew.

While he was enjoying the limelight and the success, McMaster didn't look too carefully at Hubbard's flaws. But in the sixties Hubbard was anxious to expand Scientology into Africa. Barred from South Africa, although there were Scientology centres there, he fixed on Rhodesia, and the Boomiehills Hotel.

McMaster remembers a heavy-handed attempt by Hubbard to influence Prime Minister Ian Smith while he was living in Alexander Park in Salisbury. Ron had his chauffeur drive him out in his yellow Pontiac with two bottles of pink champagne, which he had to leave with the butler because Mrs Smith would not receive him. 'There are things like protocol, you know, just general decency,' says McMaster. 'You don't just barge in on somebody like a tramp steamer misdocking. All these nuances of understanding, I began to realize, he didn't have.' With some distaste John McMaster adds, 'He told me Ian Smith was going to be shot because he was a "Suppressive". I now have no comment. But the real reason that Hubbard was kicked out of Rhodesia was that his cheques bounced.'

In the mid-sixties doors started closing in the Scientologists' faces all over the world. Whether it was from accident or design, most of the Church of Scientology target areas were in the old British Commonwealth — Australia, New Zealand, South Africa. The first door to slam was in Victoria where, in 1965, a Board of Inquiry persuaded the State legislature to pass the Psychological Practices Act which effectively outlawed Scientology in Victoria. Within half an hour,[1] Australian police had raided the Melbourne org and confiscated some 4,000 documents, personal files and books. It was now punishable by a fine of $400 to use an E-Meter unless a trained psychologist and it became a criminal offence to receive or teach Scientology materials.

The newspaper headlines at the time in Australia are a telegrammatic way of conveying the charges in the report which had been prepared by Mr Kevin Anderson QC.[2] Scientology was variously held out as 'perverted', 'a form of blackmail', 'caused delusions', 'exploited anxiety', 'a menace', 'product of an unsound mind'. This last charge referred to the diagnosis of Hubbard from a distance by Dr E. Cunningham Crax, chairman of Victoria's Mental Health Authority, who gave evidence to the Board of Inquiry that Hubbard was suffering from paranoid schizophrenia. One cannot help feeling sympathy for Scientology, which seemed to be condemned without a proper hearing, if one reads the account of the episode in Garrison's *The Hidden Story of Scientology*. He tells how Hubbard had volunteered to testify to the Board if they paid his expenses, but it is difficult to accept the bona fide of this when one reads that Garrison congratulated Hubbard on his good sense in failing to turn up in person when the Australian legal profession began discussing whether he could be charged with fraud.

The South African government was considering holding a similar Inquiry into Scientology in 1966 and McMaster was dispatched by Hubbard to trouble-shoot. The Inquiry was not held until 1969, by which time a banning order had been brought in the UK preventing leaders of Scientology from entering Britain. (It remained in force until 1980, although a report by Sir John Foster to Parliament written in 1970 and published in 1971, recommended the ban be lifted.)[3]

To summarize, the mid-sixties were a turning point for Scientology. As it expanded into Anglo-Saxon corners of the globe, it met increasing hostility from governments and the medical profession. The reaction to this from Hubbard was increased paranoia and a series of poisonous and authoritarian HCOBs poured from his pen:

26 AUGUST 1965:   The Ethics E-Meter check allowed the Ethics Officer (whose office and function had been introduced in May and June respectively) 'at any time (to) call in any staff member

---

[1] on 7 December 1965.   [2,3] *See pages 63–4.*

and do an Ethics E-Meter check . . . no question is asked . . . the EO records the position of the tone arm and the needle'.

5 AUGUST 1965:   The main characteristics of a Suppressive Person (SP) were defined and in December the 'handling' of the PTS and the suppressive group was outlined.

6 MARCH 1966:   Rewards and Penalties. How to handle Personnel and ethics matters.

27 SEPTEMBER 1966:   The 'anti-social personality', the 'anti-Scientologist'.

On and on they came, Hubbard's pen as prolific in defining, attacking, demanding as it had always been in churning out science-fiction. By September 1967 he had even defined a state of 'non-existence' for those who ran foul of his tyrannical paranoia. 'Must wear old clothes. May not bathe. Women must not wear make-up or have hair-dos. Men may not shave. No lunch-hour is given and such persons are not expected to leave the premises. Lowest pay with no bonuses.' On 1 October 1967 'Uses of Orgs' declared, 'There are two uses to which an org can be put: (1) To forward the advance of self and all dynamics towards total survival. (2) To use the great power and control of an org to defend oneself.' This was followed on 16 October by 'How to Detect SPs as an Administrator' and on 18 October by 'Penalties for Lower Conditions'. These included 'Suspension of pay and a dirty grey rag on left arm, and day and night confinement to org premises. TREASON: Black mark on left cheek.'

An enemy of Scientology became by definition a 'Suppressive Person' and thus was 'Fair Game': 'May be deprived of property or injured by any means by any Scientologist without any discipline of the Scientologists.' The Church of Scientology points out that Fair Game was cancelled by Hubbard in 1968, but it should be noted that he did this because it was causing adverse public relations, not because it was undesirable, and he added that it did not cancel any policy on the treatment or handling of a SP. In other words, business as before — and the 'business', dirty tricks, spreading false information about critics, blackmail and threats — had been pretty busy and grisly until that point. If someone was in contact with a Suppressive Person they were required to 'disconnect' from them by writing a letter. At one time it was accepted practice to publish letters of disconnection in the *Auditor* magazine, and Wallis quotes one disquieting example of a member of a family writing such a letter:

I, Heath Douglas Creer, do swear that I disavow and thoroughly disassociate myself from any covertly or overtly planned association with J. Roscoe Creer and Isabel Hodge Creer or anyone demonstrably guilty of SP acts as described in HC Policy Letters March '65. I understand that any breach of the above pledge will result in me being declared a Suppressive Person. *Signed,* H. D. Creer.

It was little wonder that Scientology acquired a reputation for being destructive of family bonds. What is probably more accurate is that Scientology is no more destructive of family connections than it is of relationships in general. What is more subtle is that once a person has made his whole life centre round the Church of Scientology, then being 'declared' (which is the verb for becoming a SP), poses a terrible threat of losing friends, job, home and perhaps family all at once. It is a chillingly effective tool for bringing dissenting voices into line.

'Out-ethics' are graded from errors to high crimes. The latter were more concerned with treason against the org itself, but ethics orders were issued holus bolus for the most trivial incidents. Failure to comply escalated the penalties and the non-conformist could soon find himself facing a Sec-Check prior to a Committee of Evidence (Comm Ev).

Among the questions asked on Sec-Checks were: 'Are you a pervert? Are you guilty of any major crimes in this lifetime? Have you been sent here knowingly to injure Scientology? Are you, or have you ever been, a Communist? Those familiar with the McCarthy witch-hunts of the early fifties will recognize the last question. But it should also be remembered that not only was the interviewee in a stressful situation but he or she was on meter and the E-Meter, as we have seen, has been compared in function closely to that of a lie-detector. In other words, a Sec-Check was a form of interrogation.

McMaster, who had been given the role of Scientology's unofficial ambassador to the United Nations, a grandiose gesture in keeping with Hubbard's pretensions, was appointed Pope of Scientology in August 1966, an event he recalls with derision. 'When Hubbard said to me, "I'm declaring you the first Pope", I thought he was joking. For me it was *never* a church. I did wear a ministerial collar at the UN and they'd say to me, "Oh, hello, Father McMaster — who would you like to see today?" and there was no problem. I was completely trusted.' Not by Hubbard, however. Even McMaster was removed from his post in September 1967, put in a state of 'non-existence' and forced to retrain.

In March 1985, McMaster had the satisfaction of returning to the stage where he was once lionized as a 'world-famous spiritual lecturer'. His audience was a new generation of Scientologists who had broken with the church. But McMaster is unaffected by this revived adulation. He returned to his shabby flat in Waterloo just as disenchanted with Scientology as the day in 1969 when he walked out on Hubbard, the man he had come to call Hitler: 'He was savage. He would just turn on people like he was a lion and we were the cubs. I had long since passed his tech but he had to be the greatest. The stuff I developed back then, they're now selling — but I don't want anything to do with being a guru or a prop for their status. I've been asked by these "opinion leaders", who are just another bunch of little Hitlers, to come in and give them credibility. They all want to be more important than anyone else.' He waves his hand dismissively and pours another drink. The aftertaste of Scientology is bitter.

John McMaster was one of the group who left Saint Hill in the mid-sixties when Scientology took to sea. The official reason given was that Hubbard had relinquished his post as Executive Director and turned over the orgs to his protégés after giving them all those HCOBs which told them everything they would need to run an org, including when to scratch their noses. His reason was that as a 'master mariner' he felt the call to go down to the sea again and had acquired a sailing yacht and also a converted channel ferry (*The Royal Scotsman*), which was renamed the *Apollo*. Another retrospective reason advanced by the Scientologists for the move to ships was that these provided the ideal training environment for the budding 'Clears'.

A more cynical view would discern that things were hotting up for Hubbard, with the possibility of governments moving against him for fraud and tax evasion. A life on the ocean-wave was a life free from restraint. Surrounded by his willing helpers, Hubbard's megalomania grew. The Commodore's Messenger Organization was set up from a corps of nubile young girls who would run errands around the ship for Hubbard. They were treated with great respect — an insult to them was an insult to Hubbard himself. He instituted a special task-force known as the Sea Organization. Its members signed 'billion-year contracts' to serve the org and Ron (presumably in this life and those to come) and dressed in naval-style uniforms with berets to match Ron's. They smoked cigarettes incessantly, just as Ron did. They talked org-speak as Ron wrote it down. And they policed one another for 'out-ethics'. Packed into the *Apollo* were five hundred of these shock troops, under the command of the 'Commodore'. If Hubbard had never tasted action during the war, he was surely determined to see some in the seaborne years that lay ahead.

Life on board the *Apollo* was a bizarre mixture of an educational cruise, being on the *Bounty* with Captain Bligh, and a version of the movie farce 'Carry on Cruising'. An inexperienced crew on a large ship can wreak havoc and the *Apollo* was no exception. Bungled navigation, incompetent and ill-trained youngsters cooped up together, it was potentially a recipe for disaster.

Ron solved the problem by making his crew into slaves. Crews mutiny, but not slaves. Penalties were draconian. 'Chain-lockering' was introduced by Hubbard as a punishment. McMaster remembers once being asked by the Master at Arms to come and help her. He pulled up the wedge from the chain-locker, a dank and unhealthy part of the ship into which offenders were flung without food as a punishment. Out crawled a little girl who turned out to be a deaf-mute who had been unable to write her name and had incurred the Commodore's wrath. The bilges were another favourite punishment cell (known as 'in the tanking'). Another penalty was being made to climb the dizzy heights to the crow's nest and stay there for a whole watch. But by far the most used (and abused) of the bully-boy tactics was 'overboarding' — Captain Hubbard's version of walking the plank. It originated in Melila when Dutchman Otto Roos, then Senior Auditor, had let a line slip as the *Apollo* was making a botched berthing. Roos is now a rich businessman. His macho manner and tough-guy approach meant that he was rarely on the side of those who were bullied. He discovered the traumatic effects of overboarding on some and declares that he ordered it stopped forthwith. But it didn't prevent McMaster being put overboard four times. The fifth and last time was on 5 November 1969. It was the last straw and when he went ashore he vowed to quit. A young lady chaplain had come to fetch McMaster from the hold because Hubbard wanted to present him with something on the poop deck to 'honour all he had done'. He says he knew right away it was a Judas kiss and Hubbard accused him of betrayal. His daughter Diana[1] (who occupied a senior position on *Apollo*) read out a list of 'high crimes' which McMaster says were all lies, and then eight burly Scientologists flung him overboard. He broke his shoulder in the fall.

1 One of Hubbard's seven children by his three marriages. (The daughter of Mary Sue.)

Otto Roos has written a diary of those years on board ship. It is peppered with org-speak, but it is a fascinating insight into the period which is now idealized by Scientologists as a golden period when Ron was developing his higher tech and sailing around the Mediterranean discovering archaeological sites where he had lived in his past lives. Extracts from Roos' diary have been widely circulated among the independent movement, since he is now among the Suppressive Persons and 'squirrels'. Here are some extracts from the Flying Dutchman's log:

'I was not all innocent and sweetness and light. Far from it. I had decided there were only two kinds of people there: those who got into the tanks and those who put them in, and that I was not going to get in, no way! . . . Having myself as a child experienced the atrocities of war, when many of my friends hadn't, I wasn't going down into those tanks. Rusty old tanks, way below in the ship, filthy bilge water, no air except via oxygen tubes, and hardly sitting height, in which sinners were put from 24 hours to a week, day and night, to hammer rust off the insides with Masters of Arms checking outside to hear if the hammering continued, and occasional food out of a bucket. This was like the concentration camps of my childhood days . . . .

'I would also have refused the crow's nest, which meant spending 4 hours in the nest and 4 hours on deck, alternating for some 84 hours. The nest, a tiny bucket at the top of the mast, too small to sit or lie in, gets cold at night. One of our SPs (named O'Keefe) had a fear of heights and virtually had to be winched up there and down again every 4 hours.

'The severe "unreasonability" started in earnest in September '67 when Non-Existence included no right to food, and Ray Thacker, huddled in a corner, would be avoided by all and occasionally thrown a crust of bread . . . .

'The Flag Orders at the time (instructions from HQ) usually dealt in "smashing THEM" (our "enemies") and smashing them we did, if not our enemies at least ourselves and most of our port relations.

'To say that LRH could not have known about this, can only be answered by "How could he not have?" on a little ship and holding all the comm. lines, after *originating* the policies. One walks around on a ship and looks. LRH has never been renowned for an inability to look.

'. . . There was continued data about SMERSH (from James Bond books), the "Enemy", bankers, psychiatrists, newspapers, port officials, etc. Port flaps were all "their" doing. Our unreasonable (and very often unseamanlike and very unprofessional) methods had "nothing to do with it". . . .

'The billion-year contract was signed of our "free will" (and some Swedes, who objected, were immediately "beached" [sent away], "never to be given upper-level materials", and "declared"). "Beaching" I have seen many times and it did not improve port relations. A beachee, put ashore with his passport and no money (except his Sea Org "pay" sometimes) to make his way home, would go to his Consulate for help and have some explaining to do. Another way to bring on the "enemy".

'Nobody ever *dared* say anything about these things and risk losing his OT levels for "making the Commodore wrong".

'Our lives were completely mapped out 24 hours a day, *personal* lives exactly prescribed, especially 2D [relations with the opposite sex] . . . The day started with "Musters", sing-songing KSW, followed by a mantra of "LRH, LRH, LRH", after which work, work, work, for little or no pay . . .'

Roos was by now a Class XII auditor, the top rank, and was auditing Hubbard himself, a dangerous task which proved his undoing.[1] The Commodore had some bad readings on the meter which were duly noted by Roos, but Hubbard would not accept these. The relationship which had flourished with LRH calling Otto up to his cabin to bounce ideas off him, deteriorated rapidly. Hubbard yelled and screamed to see his folders (which is not allowed). When Roos refused, Hubbard sent some 'hefty guys' to collect them and became even more agitated when he saw some meter-reads which did not fit in with either his 'tech' or his self-image. When Mary Sue Hubbard declared that LRH did not 'have such reads', Roos knew his number was up. MSH had previously been an ally and had ripped up the results of several 'Comm Evs' called on Roos for his sexual activities. He had been astute in avoiding supervision up to this point. Apart from LRH/MSH he had no seniors and only once had fallen foul of Hubbard when he refused a posting to run the new advanced org in Scotland and was put on pot-scrubbing duties as a penance. McMaster was the great 'tech man' and was not a senior post holder. He therefore had no hold over Roos either. Indeed,

---

[1] The auditing of members of LRH's family was case supervised by Ron himself.

the two men could not have been more different — the fey and thespian McMaster and the tough, macho Dutch ex-merchant seaman. There was no love lost between the two and McMaster even alleges that at one time Hubbard ordered Roos to kill McMaster. But they both paint a picture of the voyages of the *Apollo* which make it sound like a concentration camp afloat.

Roos left with only $100 in his pocket and made a fortune in business. His verdict on Hubbard: 'His great tragedy is that he finally penalized himself horribly by denying himself the only thing that could have saved him: his own creation — auditing.' McMaster is more jaundiced. When he left Scientology he was forcibly subjected to a Sec-Check before he threatened to call the police. He told his interrogators: 'You will never see me again. The World's First Real Clear has a right to think, doesn't he?' Indeed he does, but as McMaster finished his tale of those early years, I could not resist the conclusion that he was also the World's First Victim of Scientology.

The roll of honour of the fleet of the Church of Scientology is a glossy magazine, *High Winds*, the journal of the Sea Organization. It has a running series of 'tales from the early days of the Sea Org'. These are exploits in which the Commodore features largely. In one, he grabs the wheel and steers the *Apollo* through a jagged reef off Sicily onto which pirates are trying to lure passing ships. In another, the yacht *Enchanter* (later renamed *Diana*) is being blown in a shrieking storm onto rocks when Hubbard barks at a young sailor to climb the topmast and rig the sail while he guides the yacht clear.

I heard another story fresh from the lips of an old salt, Frank Macall, in Clearwater. He was a carpenter and second mate on the *Apollo* but served on the two other yachts — *Diana* and *Athena* (originally called *The Avon River*). Frank Macall had been in the Royal Navy when he came across Hubbard in 1966 when LRH had quit Rhodesia and was advertising in London for volunteers 'to go on an adventure'. 'He didn't tell me it was for life,' laughs Macall behind twinkling sea-blue eyes that are the acceptable face of the Sea Org. Now he works on models in the workshop at the Flag HQ in Clearwater which will adorn an exhibition celebrating the org's former life on the ocean wave.

His first voyage was to discover former lives of a different kind. *Enchanter* set off in 1966 on what Hubbard called 'Mission into Time', an attempt to trace his own past lives. 'We went to one volcanic island,' says Frank Macall, 'and LRH told me what to expect up the end of a volcanic track, but I found nothing where he said. Then on the other side I saw a little blockhouse and he reminded me how we were both there in 1682 when I was gunner's mate on his ship and he was Captain of a Portuguese man of war. Suddenly I found I had *deja vu* and could point out all the landmarks and knew every nook and cranny of the place.'

Macall remembers Hubbard as a man of many moods. 'He could dramatize them: pound the desk in fury or anoint my eyes as he did once when they were sore after welding. I'm not a worshipper or a handclapper but if there's anyone in this base with respect for LRH, it's me. Once I had spent twenty-four hours working on an engine. LRH was standing drumming his fingers, then he pushed me aside and in three or four minutes he had it working and we upped anchor. He called it "Bypass-handle" and afterwards he explained it to us.'

As Macall talked, surrounded by all the mementoes of the voyages — the model of the *Apollo*, its ship's wheel and bell — he explained why he had stayed the course in Scientology. 'If it didn't work, I wouldn't have anything to do with it, 'cos I'm a nuts and bolts man. It's the most decent, purposeful, full of integrity thing I've come across and if you comply with its laws you live in harmony with the environment. There are only a few of us old-stagers around here. We're happy to let go of the LRH thing and let him slip away.' It was hard to reconcile these tales of an old sailor with the memoirs of Roos and McMaster. Frank Macall was a gentle man whom I could not imagine thrusting deaf-mutes down into the bilges. But his view was from below decks, the gunner who looked up to his captain from 1682 onwards. Roos and McMaster had a better view from high on the bridge and had further to fall.

As mentioned earlier, the mid-sixties was a period of great fluctuation in the fortunes of the Church of Scientology. While *Apollo* was at sea, governments began to take notice of the Anderson Report of 1965 in Victoria, Australia. It was unambiguous in its denunciation of Scientology: 'Scientology is evil; its techniques evil; its practice a serious threat to the community, medically, morally, socially, and its adherents sadly deluded and mentally ill. The principles and practice of Scientology are contrary to accepted principles and practices of medicine and science and constitute a grave danger to . . . the mental health of the community. Scientology is a grave threat to family and home life.' You can't say much stronger than that. Perhaps the Church of Scientology deserves sympathy for this verdict which appears to be a case for the prosecution rather than an objective assessment. It would certainly agree that the Anderson Report influenced other governments to act who might not have done so without a clear-cut condemnation.

The Minister of Health in Britain, Mr Kenneth Robinson, addressed the House of Commons in the following terms in July 1968: 'The Government is satisfied, having reviewed all the available evidence, that Scientology is socially harmful. It alienates members of families from each other and attributes squalid and disgraceful motives to all who oppose it; its authoritarian principles and practices are a potential menace to the personality and well-being of those so deluded as to become its followers; above all, its methods can be a danger to the health of those who submit to them.' Mr Robinson went on to announce a ban on Scientology students entering the UK.

In 1968 acts were passed in South and Western Australia. In 1969 the South African government instituted a Commission of Inquiry into Scientology, and in the USA the FDA won a decision ordering the destruction of the E-Meters seized in 1963, while in the same year, 1969, the tax-exempt status of the Church of Scientology in Washington DC was revoked. Only in New Zealand was there any comfort for Hubbard and his crew when the Commission of Inquiry reported in mild tones in 1969 recommending no legislation provided Scientology kept its nose clean.

The Church of Scientology responded by modifying some of its penalties for 'lower conditions'.[1] Then it won an appeal on the FDA case in 1969 when the E-Meter was judged to be a religious artefact and as long as E-Meters were labelled as ineffective in treating illness they were permissible. In 1971 the Foster Report in Britain modified the tone of previous criticism by declaring it would be contrary to the best traditions of the Anglo-Saxon legal system to ban Scientology as in Australia. Although the British ban on foreign Scientologists working in the UK remained in force until 1980 and Scientology did not win final recognition as a religion (and therefore zero payroll tax) in Australia until 1983 by a decision of the High Court, the intense heat was off in 1970. Not so on the high seas, however, for by 1970 the shipboard operation was turning sour. The *Apollo* was meeting with a less than ecstatic reception at the Mediterranean ports at which she docked.

Hubbard was interested in establishing another centre to rival Saint

[1] revoked by stiffer penances in HCOPL dated 16 November 1971.

early picture of L. Ron Hubbard

Above: Saint Hill Manor, East Grinste
Sussex with castle complex, designed b
L. Ron Hubbard, on the left

Left: London HQ of the Church of
Scientology in Tottenham Court Roac

ove: Candacraig House, Strathdon, tland

Below: Robin Scott, his wife Adrienne and their family

Above: View of Municipal Buildings, Clearwater, from the Penthouse at the Fort Harrison Hotel, with Bay of Tampa in background

Below: The author examining an E-Meter at Flag HQ

Right: Room stocked with confidential pc folders in 'Flag HQ' (Fort Harrison Hotel, Clearwater)

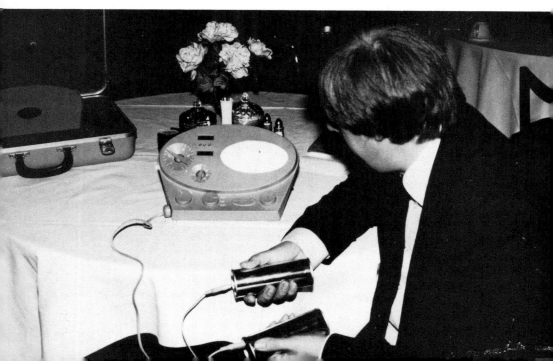

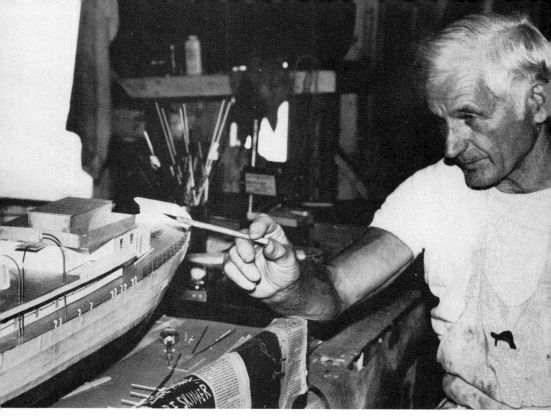

Above and left: 'Old salt', Frank McCa
remembering past voyages with a mod
of *Apollo* and ship's wheel

Right: Hubbard and film crew workin
Southern California in the late seventie
The youth directly below Hubbard is
David Miscavige

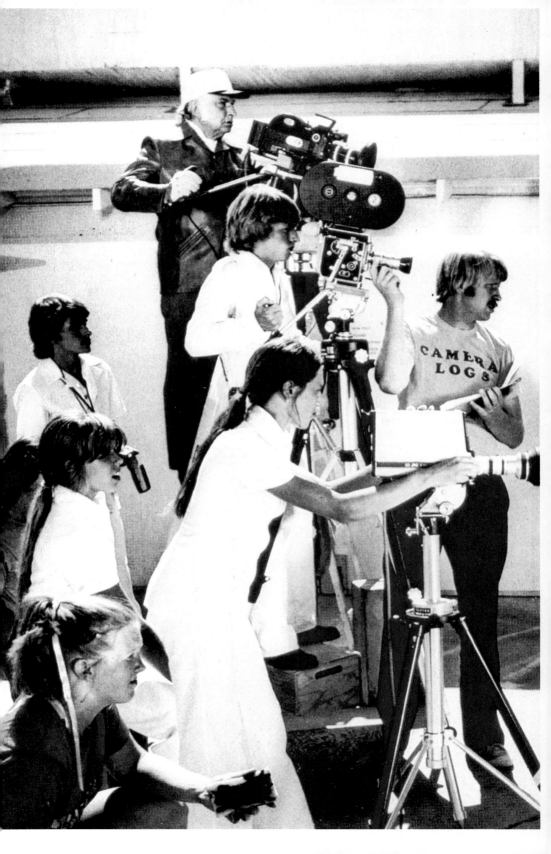

Hubbard on location

Hill, but the British ban prevented it being in the UK. He was convicted *in absentia* of fraud in France. The IRS were following their success in wiping out the tax-exempt status of the founding Church of Scientology in Washington DC by looking into the affairs of the Church of Scientology (California Corporation) which was a thriving centre and one through which funds were channelled to the *Apollo*. The other areas in which the orgs were strong, as we have just seen, were subject to government interference. Hubbard did two things: (1) To handle the money, he set up the RRF (Religious Research Foundation) in Luxemburg with bank accounts there. Money was channelled there, especially the income from non-US nationals and then onto the *Apollo*. Those who imagine that Hubbard's resignation as Executive Director and 'Supreme Commander' in 1966 was anything other than a cosmetic gesture were deluding themselves. LRH was very much in charge and that meant especially of the money. (In a later chapter we shall look at this highly important factor in Scientology.) (2) Hubbard then looked around the Mediterranean for a Mecca and intuitively he turned for Greece, from whence the very names of his ships were derived. It was hoped to establish a 'University of Philosophy' in Corfu, but the project blew up in the church's face when unjustified claims of Greek government support were made. The Scientologists claim that their enemies in the USA and Britain tainted them with black propaganda. A less polite version is that the Church of Scientology could not resist pulling a few dirty tricks and the Greeks saw through its methods. The Sea Org fleet was ordered out of Corfu ignominiously in March 1970 halfway through a refit.

The next prospect was Tangier in Morocco. The Sea Org fleet stayed in the Western Mediterranean, also sailing to Portugal, the Canaries and Spain in this period. The *Apollo* went into dry dock in Lisbon in 1972 and on 3 December 1972 Hubbard and his wife were given twenty-four hours to leave Tangier. They flew to Lisbon but there Hubbard was advised that he could be extradited to France following the fraud case brought in his absence, so he flew back to the United States and went into hiding with his medical officer Jim Dincalci in an apartment in the suburb of Queens, NY City.

Hubbard was not in good health but managed to work on several 'Operations' to get back at the Enemy, among them 'Operation Snow White' (see p. 79). He returned to the *Apollo* in September 1973 and she sailed mainly in the East Atlantic.

In October 1974 the *Apollo* sailed into Madeira off the Canary Islands where the 'Apollo Allstars' planned to take part in a rock festival. But the plan went horribly wrong. A crowd stormed the ship believing that she was part of a cover operation for the CIA, and the *Apollo* was forced to put to sea, with one crew member killed in the fracas.

The ship crossed the Atlantic and arrived off South Carolina, but could not berth because the FBI were waiting. She went on to Nassau, then Curaçao, where in 1975 Hubbard suffered a stroke and was taken ashore to the Hilton Hotel in Cabana. The West Indies were not happy to receive the *Apollo*. The worldwide reputation of the Church of Scientology was bad enough but unstable governments of small islands needed a boat-load of Scientologists pouring ashore like they needed a hole in the head. Jim Jones found Guyana as a home for his deadly cult, but for Hubbard there was to be no bolt-hole. It was then that he devised a better plan. He would take over a whole town in his own country, the United States.

4 God's Admiralty

THE CENTRE of Florida's Suncoast is the beautiful bay which stretches out from the town of Tampa. On its southern branch is St Petersburg where I once watched the most lurid sunset I have ever seen flood the sky with colour. Hours earlier a storm in the Gulf of Mexico had been signposted by a 'twister' which moved menacingly across the horizon. On the north of the bay of Tampa is the sleepy town of Clearwater. In 1975 its mainly retired community, many of whom were Baptists, were feeling a chill wind of recession in the tourist trade. The splendid Fort Harrison Hotel run by the Jack Tar organization was for sale in the downtown area around the waterfront overlooking the municipal buildings which administered the town — incorporated under a Home Rule Charter of the State of Florida. A block away was the former Bank of Clearwater building which was also for sale. Another few blocks away was the Sandcastle Motel, which was also feeling the pinch.

On 27 October 1975, the Fort Harrison Hotel was purchased by Southern Land Sales and Development Corporation for $2.3 million hard cash, and a few days later the corporation acquired the bank building for $550,000. Then a spokesman for United Churches of Florida stepped up to say that his organization was to be leased the buildings to hold ecumenical seminars for laymen of all faiths. Jack Tar Hotels were still puzzled when they were not even given a telephone number by the mysterious Southern Land Sales organization. They were soon to discover that both it and United Churches of Florida were fronts for the Church of Scientology.

Part of the plan in acquiring the new headquarters in Florida was to provide a 'dormant Corp' into which the assets and cash of the Church of Scientology of California could be siphoned off should they be seized or wiped out by the IRS in California, which still controlled the purse-strings. Another purpose was to provide a 'Flag Land Base' which would take over the functions of the harassed *Apollo*.

There was another policy which was the brain-child of the new Guardians' Office. This was to establish the credibility of United Churches with opinion leaders in the local community. A directive ordered Scientologists to 'locate opinion leaders — then their enemies, the dirt, scandal, vested interests, crimes of the enemies . . . then turn this information over to UC who will approach the opinion leader and get his agreement to look into a specific subject. . . . UC then discovers the scandal and turns it over to the opinion leader for his use.' An actual example was given of an enemy of one mayor who was a secret child-molester in the local park: the UC would demand a 'clean up the park campaign' which would just happen to disclose this dirt. This information would then be handed to the mayor on a plate. With friends like that, you might ask, what opinion leader needed enemies?

This ploy rebounded rather badly on the Church of Scientology. Clearwater's Mayor, Gabriel Cazares, was none too impressed by the secrecy of the 'United Churches' operation. 'I am discomfited by the increasing visibility of security personnel armed with billyclubs and mace, employed by the United Churches of Florida,' said the Mayor. 'I am unable to understand why this degree of security is required by a religious organization.'

On 28 January 1976, Arthur J. Maren of the Church of Scientology arrived in Clearwater and announced that the church was the real buyer of the Fort Harrison Hotel. The Church of Scientology did not wish to overshadow the good intentions of the United Churches, said Mr Maren. A public meeting was held at which the Church of Scientology outlined its high moral principles. But concealed behind this velvet voice was the steely intention to silence Mayor Cazares. On 6 February, just over a week after Maren came to town, a $1 million lawsuit was filed against the Mayor for libel, slander and violation of the church's civil rights. It didn't stop there. Behind the scenes a memo was circulating among Scientologists. It read: 'SITUATION: set of entheta (unfavourable) articles connection UC and LRH breaking now in Flag area papers. WHY: Unhandled enemies; possible plant and out-security. HANDLED: Collections and ops underway on reporters Orsini, Sableman and Snyder (radio broadcaster). Results of ops not in yet . . .'

The operations consisted of smear-tactics against the journalists who had been investigating the Church of Scientology. 'Operation

Bunny Bust' directed against reporter Bette Orsini of the *St Petersburg Times* consisted of planting allegations that her husband was involved in fraud activities in the charity for which he worked. There was no substance in these allegations. Indeed, they had the opposite effect. The newspapers filed a suit to prevent the church from harassing their reporters and strengthened their resolve to expose as much of the Church of Scientology's activities as possible. It was not until several years later that the documents emerged which showed conclusively that the smear-campaigns were authorized and directed by the Church of Scientology; otherwise they might have been explained as over-zealous conduct by paranoid Scientologists coming ashore from the *Apollo*, which had landed at Daytona Beach. Another suggestion was that dirt might be procured on the Chairman of the *St Petersburg Times* by tapping his servants. But the most vicious campaign was that directed at Mayor Cazares.

The first step in the campaign was a letter which purported to be from one of the Mayor's supporters and was sent to downtown businesses, especially the Jewish ones. 'God bless the Mayor' it began and went on to congratulate Cazares on his stand against Scientology, concluding: 'What we should do is make sure no more undesirables move into Clearwater. We kept the Miami Jews from turning beautiful Clearwater into Miami Beach. The blacks are decent and know their place . . .' That was just for starters. The next ploy was to infiltrate a forged document into a Mexican licence bureau which would 'prove' that Cazares was bigamously married to his present wife. Mrs Cazares was thus drawn into the tangled web. 'We'd been married twenty-nine years. Suddenly I was getting all kinds of mysterious phone-calls: girls calling "Is Gabe there?", telling me there's something personal between "he and me". Asking me if I knew where — "Do you know where Gabe is now?" — Things like that, you know.'

There was no end to the attempts to silence Gabriel's horn. In February 1976 the possibility of trawling Cazares' school records was being looked into. A few weeks later they schemed to present him as pro-Castro to the many Cuban exiles who live in Florida. The darkest operation yet was mounted in March 1976 when the Mayor went to Washington for a national conference of mayors. He was met by Joseph Alesi posing as a reporter and was introduced to Sharon Thomas who offered to show him Washington. As Cazares and Thomas were driving along, she hit a pedestrian (Church of Scientology agent Mike Meisner who feigned injury) and drove on. Following the hit-and-run 'accident', a church memo gleefully recorded 'I should think the Mayor's political days are at an end'. That was a very real possibility, for Cazares was by this time a Democratic candidate for the congressional seat held by Republican representative Bill Young.

Over lunch, Young's administrative assistant was offered information which could damage Cazares' campaign by a Church of Scientology PR official. He refused the offer. So on 12 July, 'Operation Keller' went into action to 'create havoc and political decay for Cazares'. Fake letters from 'Sharon T.' were mailed to political leaders in Pinellas County stating that Cazares had been involved in a hit-and-run accident in Washington. Cazares asked the FBI to investigate. Meanwhile, Young received a letter saying that the 'Sharon T.' letter was really authorized by the Cazares campaign in an attempt to implicate him in dirty tricks. Let us just recap that sequence since it almost defies credibility. The Guardians' Office of Scientology faked a hit-and-run accident implicating Cazares and leaked this information to his opponents, then wrote to these opponents double-bluffing them into thinking that Cazares had faked it in order to discredit them. Iago was a goody-goody compared to this lot.

In October, church agent Dick Weigand reported to his boss, Mo Budlong: 'A recent poll conducted by the *Clearwater Sun* received phoney responses from the public, generated covertly, which showed that his (Cazares') opponent had a crushing lead on him.' On 3 November 1976 a triumphant memo from Joe Lisa to Duke Snider recorded that Cazares had been defeated in the congressional race as a result of Guardian Order 398 — an operation to create strife between Cazares and the city commission; to place a church agent in his campaign organization to cause problems ('spreading rumours in his camp').

It was not the first nor the last time that infiltration had been practised by the Church of Scientology. Meisner was currently running agent 'Silver' (alias Gerald Bennett Wolfe) who had been employed as a clerk-typist at the Inland Revenue Service (IRS) since 1974. *Femme fatale* Sharon Thomas had got a job at the Justice Department in January 1976 at Meisner's instigation. Back at 'Flag' in Clearwater, there was also a plant in the *Clearwater Sun* newspaper office: June Byrne who had been undercover at the AMA (American Medical Association) and now was feeding the church daily reports on the anti-Scientology activities of the paper. On 17 March 1976 she reported that Assistant City Editor Tom Coat was taking a Scientology course at the Tampa mission under cover as a freelance photographer. Coat was exposed by the church who issued a Press release and followed it with a $250,000 lawsuit against Coat and the *Sun*. June Byrne duly reported that Coat had heard about the lawsuit on his car radio and had appeared in the office in a state of severe shock.

All this activity by the Guardians' Office did not win respectability for the Church of Scientology; nor did it win the war of words. But if it did not achieve a truce, it was at least partly effective in securing a ceasefire from many of the church's opponents. Broadcaster Bob Snyder of the WDCL radio station was fired after a $5 million lawsuit was threatened against the station for anti-Scientology broadcasts he was making. The station reinstated him but with a proviso that he did not discuss Scientology on the air.

The church's libel action against Cazares was dismissed by Judge Ben Krentzmann in Tampa in the spring of 1977 and it later dropped two other lawsuits and Cazares withdrew *his* suit against the church. The *Clearwater Sun* had planned a book on Scientology but this did not appear. The *St Petersburg Times* did not pursue its lawsuit in order to protect the slender financial resources of the Easter Seal Society, the charity for which reporter Bette Orsini's husband worked, which would have been drawn into the case. However, the *St Petersburg Times* did publish a 25c booklet which details most of the events which have just been described. They were able to do so when many of the 48,149 internal Church of Scientology documents which were seized in an FBI raid in 1977 on the Washington org, were made public and nine senior Scientologists were sent to jail.

Books about Scientology have a greater permanency than newspaper articles and therefore it should not come as a surprise that vigorous smear-campaigns have been conducted against the authors of such investigations. The first book to run foul of the church was *The Scandal of Scientology* by journalist Paulette Cooper, which was written in 1971. To try to silence her, the Church of Scientology cooked up a scheme to steal some of her stationery and make it appear that she had sent them two bomb threats. One of the forgeries read: 'James, this is the last time I'm warning you. I don't know why I'm doing this but you're all out to get me and I'll give you one week before Scientology is an exploding volcano. I'll knock you out if my friends won't.' The Scientologists themselves then called in the police and as a result Paulette Cooper was arrested and indicted on three counts, facing up to fifteen years in jail if convicted. She told the '60 Minutes' television programme in April 1980: 'The whole ordeal fighting these charges took eight months. It cost me $19,000 in legal fees. I went into such a depression. I couldn't eat. I couldn't sleep. I couldn't write. I went down to 83 pounds. Finally I took and passed a sodium pentothal — or truth serum — test and the Government dropped the charges against me in 1975.' Further tactics were to write her phone number and obscene graffiti on walls in New York City where she lives, and put her name on pornographic mailing lists.

When the Clearwater scandal broke and she was booked to appear in Florida at broadcaster Snyder's invitation, the church decided to 'handle' its old nemesis in a new operation entitled 'Freakout'. Its goal was 'to get P.C. incarcerated in a mental institution or jail or at least hit her so hard that she drops her attacks'. Phase one involved telephone threats to Arab consulates by a voice impersonator (Ms Cooper is Jewish). Phase two, sending a threatening letter along the old bomb-hoax lines to such a consulate. Phase three, an impersonator would publicly threaten the President and Henry Kissinger while another Scientologist would tip off the authorities. Phase four, agents who had ingratiated themselves with Cooper (she at one time apparently had a relationship with a Church of Scientology man who was acting as an undercover agent) would help assess the success of the plan and if necessary notepaper bearing her fingerprints would be typed over with a bomb threat to Kissinger.

'Operation Freakout', however, didn't get off the ground. Although she appeared in the television programme in 1980 and at the Clearwater hearing instigated by attorney Michael Flynn, Cooper eventually signed a truce with Scientology and was offered a settlement (see pages 142–3). For some of the campaigners, the hassle, the wounds, the possibility that justice may not be done, makes them back off.

Sparkling Clearwater has not forgotten the day the Scientologists came to town. Those initial years when the cargo of frenzied 'Clears' came pouring ashore and began their covert operations against anyone who stood in their way, gave way to a period when the focus of church activity shifted to the West coast. Hubbard was present in Clearwater during the 'United Churches of Florida' ploy, staying at a condominium in Dunedin. He was worried about his health and had with him two personal physicians, Jim Dincalci, who had accompanied him to Washington DC in March 1976, and Kima Douglas. There is no reason to suppose he was not fully aware of all the operations being conducted against opponents. His wife, Mary Sue Hubbard, was responsible for instigating many of them and, as we shall see shortly, her appetite for dirty tricks was not confined to

Clearwater. When the LRH entourage moved away and the local opposition had passed its peak in 1976, Clearwater was still nominally the HQ of Scientology in the USA. It was here that the highest levels of the 'tech' were delivered and therefore it was here that the *crème de la crème* of Scientology's aspiring thetans came to be trained and put through their paces. They stayed in the Fort Harrison with their families or in the Sandcastle Motel and when Hubbard released the 'New Era Dianetics' courses in 1978, it was regarded as the 'top tech terminal'. This event, incidentally, was known as The Year of Technical Breakthroughs, and in org-speak as 'NOTS A.D.28'.

My own visit to Flag, as Clearwater is known, took place in a calmer climate. Young families played around in the courtyard of new accommodation at the rear of the Fort Harrison. The auditing rooms buzzed with activity and echoed to accents from all round the globe. Upstairs in the Fort Harrison a careful restoration had taken place of the Crystal Ballroom once used by citizens of Clearwater for big functions and high-school graduations. In a careful piece of fence-mending the Scientologists had not only restored it but had opened it to public hire for functions. And a good job they have made too. The Robert Adam style elliptical room with its pink carpet woven in Ulster at $32 per square yard is justifiably the pride and joy of Karen Valles who showed me round. There was an exhibition on show of work by artists who were Scientologists and much among it that would have no trouble in competing among the best in an open exhibition. The posters of Gottfried Helnwein impressed me greatly and Karen was at pains to point out that HCOBs on the subject of art were used in fostering creativity. 'What LRH did was to lay out "importances" which make it much easier to grasp the appropriate art form.' I mumbled polite assent and we went up to the penthouse which was being refurbished. It overlooks the City Hall in Clearwater, Mayor Cazares' old perch. His successor, Mayor (Mrs) Kathy Kelly, enjoys a less hostile relationship with the Church of Scientology but it is still not without its prickly areas.

In September 1984, in the week in which I visited Clearwater, the city had just announced proposed regulations which would clear the downtown area of tax-exempt organizations — among which the Church of Scientology, as a religious foundation, numbered significantly. Eight of Scientology's ten properties in the town were in that area. It would have moved the ground literally from under the church's feet in Florida. A spokesman for Clearwater City denied that the proposal was aimed specifically at the Church of Scientology. He said that Clearwater needed tax dollars to develop downtown and that these were not forthcoming from tax-exempt organizations.

It was not the first time the city had moved to rid itself of the Scientologists. In spring 1982 it invited Boston attorney Michael Flynn, scourge of Scientology in the United States, to present a series of hearings on the church. For five days a series of witnesses, including Cazares, Paulette Cooper and Hubbard's estranged son Ronald (alias DeWolf), testified to the blacker side of the Church of Scientology. The church declined to participate since it argued it could not cross-examine the witnesses and could only put its case after Flynn had poisoned the ground. The five days were effectively used by Flynn and despite the cost of $160,000 for the hearings he left the Clearwater authority a blueprint with which to eradicate Scientology from its doorstep.

The city began by putting pressure on the Church of Scientology to grant refunds to dissatisfied clients. But by far the most controversial move was the proposed Clearwater 'Charitable Solicitation Ordinance' which would enable the authorities to regulate the activities of any such organization collecting more than $10,000 annually. Flag, one-time jewel in the Scientology crown, earned the Church of Scientology a thousand times that amount. The Scientologists appealed against the ordinance to the courts on the grounds that it violated the First Amendment to the US Constitution guaranteeing freedom of religion. Judge Jovachivech at first saw it that way too, but she changed her mind four months later and held that the proposed ordinance was indeed constitutional and advised both sides that they could appeal. That is where the case was in 1986 (along with many others involving the Church of Scientology and its opponents) in a legal limbo that drags on from year to year.

Another move by the city administrators was to hold a referendum to approve a Bay Front Development which would gobble up the Sandcastle Motel. The city has not forgiven nor forgotten the events of 1976, despite vigorous efforts by officials of the Church of Scientology to make amends.

As I walked from the Fort Harrison to the Sandcastle Motel with Public Affairs Director, former lawyer Richard ('Rich') Haworth, we stopped at a pedestrian crossing with no cars in sight. I was about to proceed but he waited quietly for the green light to show. He explained that he and other Scientologists now have to be extra diligent in observing the law. 'We live in a goldfish bowl here. If a Scientologist is walking down the street wearing socks of different colours, then somebody will notice.'

As we swam up and down the Sandcastle Motel swimming-pool and youthful Scientologists resident for courses walked round, Rich Haworth explained to me why being a Scientologist was important to him. 'In the day that the button is to be pushed, it's important that the guy is a "Clear", then it will only be pushed in a way that is unavoidable. It's basically survival that we're talking about. I can do more for the survival of the planet by being here in the Church of Scientology Public Affairs Department than practising law. It's dying with your boots on rather than being a spectator. Spectatorism is rampant in the media and people adopt "I don't have an opinion" as a way of life. Flynn's products are destruction and death. He doesn't put anything in place of what he's destroying. Handling Flynn is counterproductive,' Rich Haworth continued. 'The main show is what is going to improve people and that is the show we're going to keep on the road. We have a number of improved people working in society to improve it. That's what we're about.'

Would even arch-enemy Flynn be capable of redemption, I cheekily asked. 'Yes,' said Rich with a smile, 'but an individual's improvement depends on the overts he's committed and Flynn would have a long way to audit. Scientologists can pick themselves up by their bootstraps but if it weren't for the integrity of what LRH did we couldn't do that. One of the real tragedies of psychology is Situation Ethics and people get lost in a conflicting mass of ideas of what is right and wrong. Whereas LRH says if your action does the greatest good for the greatest number of Dynamics then it's right.' I seemed to recall that it was John Stuart Mill who said it, not Hubbard, and that it was called Utilitarianism.

Back at lunch in the Fort Harrison (a rather indifferent selection of salads at high prices), I was introduced to two Class XII auditors, the top-rank supervisors of the 'tech'. They both had somewhat intense stares and as they seemed to use their eyeballs rather more than their tongues, lunch was not a coruscating display of wit and wisdom. The only drop of blood I managed to squeeze out of these stony stares was from John Eastment, who has a masters degree in Electrical Engineering. What were the kind of things that auditing could solve, I asked, and was told that if there was a marital problem it could be chased back to source. Example? Bloop, bloop went the eyes. Apparently if the wife had burnt the toast and her husband had shouted at her, that could be an engram that was choking the relationship. It would have to be audited out. We finished lunch with me reflecting that it was no wonder that people ran up so many hours of costly auditing trying to get a little back-chat from Class XII auditors.

On the way out of the Fort Harrison I was permitted to peek into a room where the personal folders are kept, containing all the secrets disclosed during auditing. The confessions, the guilty responses squeezed out during 'Sec Checks' were all there. Security is very tight, Rich explained. No one but your personal auditor and case supervisor would be allowed to see the contents of one of these folders. 'The secrets of the auditing room are as sacrosanct as the secrets of the confession box.'

In the evening it was time for a film-show in the Fort Harrison. A tape-slide presentation of the life of L. Ron Hubbard was showing and I was seated in the back row. Childhood pictures of Ron were shown as the legends about him were regailed by the narrator. 'I'm not like the other kids, not me, you bet at all,' he wrote in a song at the age of sixteen, ''cos my dad's a naval man.' As a Scout he met the President of the US, Calvin Coolidge, we were told, and was disappointed he had to go to the President and not the other way around. He noted that the President had a limp handshake. 'I was the only Scout to have made the President wince,' noted Ron in his diary, which is strangely the only document to have recorded the meeting. In Guam, when a youth in 1928, his red hair attracted stares from the natives. Then he was told that everyone who had red hair was made a king. He recorded himself in his diary as 'H.M. the Duke of Guam'. Such blatant immodesty was presented in such a way that the person already devoted to Hubbard would smile indulgently with the benefit of hindsight at these glimpses of destiny granted to the hero.

The tape-slide show ended with Ron signing off in a somewhat final manner in a message recorded in Las Palmas in 1967: 'I have borne it too long alone. . . . I need your help . . . Goodbye for now. I will see you at the line at the other end of the Bridge. . . .' This message was made at a time when Ron was supposed to have relinquished control over Scientology. As we have seen, it was not so at that time. He was supposed to be in seclusion so that he could devote himself to writing and this is still the answer given to those who enquire why he disappeared from view in 1980.

After the film-show I chatted to an old salt, Wally Burgess from Australia, who has been a Scientologist since 1954 and voyaged on the *Apollo*. He was tough, weatherbeaten and bald. The hour was late but he was there in uniform as if the Fort Harrison and 'Flag' were still at sea and he was on watch. The hooded eyes watched me shrewdly. 'The greatest single difficulty we have is in stating the man's [LRH] abilities in such a way that people will listen. He's such a smart fella,' said Wally the Aussie. 'We probably err in trying to pass on too much to the uninitiated. You've gotta approach it on a gradient that he can accept. When I began in 1954 I could never have accepted my present understanding of what he has achieved.' This all-will-be-revealed-when-you're-ready approach enhances the mystique for many. But it also explains why there are so many pleasant and apparently open people within Scientology.

Breakfast at the Sandcastle Motel with Rich Haworth was memorable for three things. First, the splendid sensation of breakfasting alfresco overlooking the Clearwater harbour. Secondly, the waffles dripping with maple syrup which I ordered with my mixed grill. Third, the curious little note which came with the bill. It was a score-sheet for our attractive waitress. I did not have to mark her feminine attributes but her performance as a waitress out of ten. This, Rich Haworth explained, was standard throughout Scientology. Everyone is assessed on their performance and it is a measure of their effectiveness in following the 'tech'. Mission holders and auditors are assessed on how many people they are 'flowing up the Bridge'. Their 'stats' can be written in dollars and figures, but a waitress needs another objective measure. My subjective assessment would be added to that of others and constitute her 'stats' for performance purposes. Rich gave her a score of ten. After such a breakfast could I do anything but follow his lead? However, when we then went up to my room I found an assessment sheet from the maid asking me to give her some stats. The room seemed tidy but, alas, the toilet remained unflushed. I jokingly remarked that it was good to find Scientological maids were as imperfect as others. 'Tell her why,' said Rich earnestly. 'She'd appreciate that.' Whether or not my reminder about the toilet-bowl helped my room-maid to edge an inch further to the state of 'Clear', I have no idea, but I departed sparkling Clearwater with a flat feeling.

My courteous host was within the week promoted from Public Affairs to an executive post at 'Flag', then within a month was transferred to the Los Angeles HQ where his expertise as a lawyer would presumably come in handy since the Church of Scientology was rumoured to be spending in excess of $1.5 million a month in legal fees during 1984. As in the case of members of the armed services, he was given a posting.

Staff members in Scientology are like Navy personnel at sea. They are on call for duty at all hours without overtime and the hours are often long. A typical day is 9.15 a.m to 11 p.m. While every effort is made to post husbands and wives to the same org, they can spend months with several thousand miles between them as they fulfil their duties. While it is as hierarchical as the Navy on which it is modelled, the Sea Org could never be accused of transgressing Equal Rights for Women. Scientology is probably unique in the proportion of women in influential posts. Prime among them is Hubbard's wife, Mary Sue, who competed with her husband in the invention of bigger and better dirty tricks when she headed the Guardians' Office.

Although Rich Haworth and his colleagues in Public Affairs presented a most acceptable face of Scientology, the documents do not lie. The documents in question were among the 48,149 removed from Church of Scientology premises in Los Angeles and Washington on 8 July 1977 by FBI agents. They showed an amazingly successful campaign to infiltrate government agencies, place disinformation and gather blackmail material on both enemies and on their own agents. In retrospect the arrests and convictions which followed have been portrayed as the bringing to book of a few black sheep who had strayed in attempting to counteract false reports which the Government harboured in opposing Scientology. Nothing could be further from the truth. It was the Church of Scientology which was charged with inserting false reports in these agencies. The eleven conspirators indicted were the top rank of the Guardians' Office, the senior people in administering Hubbard's 'tech', and included his own wife.

The blueprint for this campaign was written by Mary Sue Hubbard on 16 December 1969. It is Guardian Order (GO)121669. Here are some excerpts: 'MAJOR TARGET: To use any and all means to detect any infiltration, double-agent or disaffected staff member, Scientologist or relatives of Scientologists and by any and all means to render null any harm such may have rendered Scientology. . . . To establish intelligence files on all such persons . . . to make full use of all files on the organization to effect your major target. These include personnel files, Ethics files, dead files, central files, training files, PROCESSING FILES and requests for refunds' [my caps]. This document concludes: 'This is a continuing program on which projects will be issued from time to time.' It was signed MARY SUE HUBBARD. This was the foundation-stone on which the Operations against Cazares and the others were built. But once it had been operating for a few years, there were many things done in its furtherance which broke the law.

Any evidence linking the Hubbards to these activities was potential dynamite. To counteract it, several 'Operations' were developed. The first of these, 'Operation Snow White', was prepared by Hubbard himself while in hiding in an apartment in Queens, NY City with Jim Dincalci in 1973 while he was feeling ill and keeping low from the possibility of extradition to face the French anti-Church of Scientology case. By 1977 there were three others. The first of these was an early-warning system which would alert the Guardians to any attempt to indict or file a suit against Hubbard personally and which would raise his 'level of personal security immediately very high', i.e. enable him to dodge the authorities. The early-warning system was to be activated by any of the various agents of the Guardians planted in various government agencies including the IRS. There was also 'Operation Bulldozer Leak' which was designed to use these same agents to spread the rumour that Hubbard was no longer in charge of or responsible for the doings of the Church of Scientology. But by far the biggest parcel of dynamite was the 'Red Box system' introduced on 25 March 1977. The Red Box in question was a container at all orgs which was to be removed by a designated person in the event of a raid. Red Box material was defined as: '(a) Proof that a Scientologist is involved in criminal activities; (b) anything illegal that incriminates MSH/LRH (the Hubbards).' Also included were details about any operations against government groups or persons, or which contained illegal activities and the details of confidential financial accounts. Among those 48,149 documents was a lot of Red Box material.

The events which led up to the FBI raid were straight out of the Watergate scenario and became known as 'Silvergate'. In 1976 the Church of Scientology had used its agent 'Silver' inside the IRS to obtain several intelligence files on celebrities, politicians and big names. This originated in GO 1361 dated 4 January 1976, but it has never been made clear whether the purpose of gathering these files was to embarrass the IRS by making them public or to use them against the people concerned. Among the files stolen were those on California Governor Edmund Brown; Los Angeles mayor Tom Bradley and his wife; singer Frank Sinatra and actor John Wayne, among others. The Deputy Guardian (Information) Dick Weigand sent the files to Deputy Guardian (US) Henning Heldt who returned them as they were 'too hot to have in my files'.

In March 1976 Guardian agent Mike Meisner (fresh from being 'run over' by Sharon Thomas's car in Rock Creek Park, Washington), met agent Gerald Bennett Wolfe, who was undercover as 'Silver' in the

IRS building at 1111 Constitution Ave, Washington NY. They entered the building in the evening and flashed Wolfe's ID card at the security man. Inside, they forced open the door of the room used to produce ID cards. While Meisner thumbed through the book of instructions for the photographic machine, Wolfe typed fictitious names on four blank cards and they made themselves fake ID cards, two for each of them. Meisner took the false name of 'John Foster'. Then they vanished into the night. In April the two men returned to the office of Thomas Crate, an auditor who had tax records of LRH and MSH, but found the door locked and persuaded a suspicious cleaning lady to open it. She obliged on two other occasions while they photocopied the files before returning them to Crate's office.

Meanwhile, Sharon Thomas was now in place in the Justice Department where she had obtained a job as secretary to attorney Paul Figley who dealt with Freedom of Information Act cases. (The Church of Scientology was currently pursuing an FOI lawsuit against the Energy Research and Development Administration and she was churning out photocopies of correspondence and other material to pass to her bosses in the GO.)

The Guardians were pretty pleased with themselves. However, disaster struck on 11 June. Meisner and Wolfe were sitting in the library of the US Courthouse at the foot of Capitol Hill, waiting for the cleaners to vacate the office of Nathan Dodell, an old Church of Scientology foe whose personal file they were after in order to devise an operation to remove him as Assistant US Attorney for the District of Columbia. But a suspicious librarian summoned a couple of FBI agents and the two Guardians soon found themselves explaining to Special Agent Christine Hansen that they had been in the library to do legal research and to use the photocopy machine. Meisner asked if they were under arrest and when she said no, they left.

Meisner flew to California the next day to report to the Guardians' Office who decided that a rescue operation should be mounted. The cover-up operation was planned in Los Angeles at the offices of the Guardians in Fifield Manor. After reading Meisner's report, Guardians Heldt and Snider were of the opinion that Wolfe and Meisner should be spirited away beyond the reach of the FBI. Then they would not have to face charges and the matter would be closed. Dick Weigand argued that, on the contrary, it would spur the FBI to look more closely into the affairs of the Guardians' Office. He put forward a plan which involved Wolfe's pleading guilty to possessing a false ID, and invented a false cover story. 'John Foster', Wolfe would say, was someone he had met for a few drinks in a bar and who offered to teach him how to undertake legal research. While pursuing this ploy, and under the influence of alcohol, they had seen the room in the Courthouse in which ID cards were made and had entered and made themselves the cards for a 'lark'. Since they had only met in the bar, Wolfe was unable to contact Foster again and did not know where he lived. Once Wolfe was given a minor sentence, Meisner could appear and plead guilty. That way the Church of Scientology would not be brought into matters at all.

Thus on 14 June, Weigand's secretary Janet Finn came to Meisner's motel room in Los Angeles, cut his hair, dyed it, shaved off his moustache and arranged for him to have soft contact lenses fitted. Suitably disguised, he slipped undercover and moved into Weigand's apartment. Back in Washington, Wolfe made sure that any mention of Meisner in the Guardians' Office was removed from the files. Wolfe was arrested on 30 June by Christine Hansen and duly told his version of the cover story. On 28 July 1976 Wolfe appeared before a magistrate who bound him over for action by the Grand Jury. However, to the consternation of the Guardians, a few days later on 5 August a warrant was issued for the arrest of one Michael Meisner.

Weigand was mystified how the FBI knew Meisner's true identity. He could only speculate in a report to Guardian supremo, Mary Sue Hubbard, that the FBI had located his former apartment house and shown his photo to a neighbour. He suggested several courses of action: further disguise for Meisner and the possibility of moving him out of the country. Mary Sue Hubbard replied: 'On getting him abroad, unless you have a good ID for him different than his own, it might be dangerous. He would better be "lost" in some large city where it would be difficult to find him.' Would it be possible to get Meisner an alibi she asked Weigand, in a letter dated 18 September. Weigand pointed out there would be difficulties. It would come down to 'our word against two FBI agents, cleaners and guards plus handwriting experts . . . fingerprint experts.' In a letter of 22 September, he favoured getting Meisner out of the country for five years until the statute of limitations had expired (an erroneous assumption as it turned out). He added ominously, 'There would be attempts to get him to turn or otherwise implicate us or others in various wrong-doings.' But Meisner was having none of it. He did not want to leave the country. He was becoming restive and missing his wife and children. Mary Sue Hubbard suggested a cold-blooded alternative which involved portraying Meisner as jealous of his wife's productivity within the Church of Scientology, implying that he had organized the burglary in a fit of jealous pique. Clearly Meisner was expendable in an effort to avoid the Church of Scientology taking responsibility for agents acting under its instructions.

A trail was also laid by the Guardians using one of their Scientologists who was a lieutenant in the San Diego Police Force. Lt. Warren Young requested information regarding the arrest-warrant for Meisner from the National Crime Information Center computer. When Special Agent Christine Hansen ordered an investigation into why San Diego were interested, Lt. Young informed the FBI that he had arrested Meisner the previous day on a traffic offence. Although in fact Meisner had never been to San Diego, the FBI were diverted by following the false trail and Weigand remarked with satisfaction that this 'can't help but help us, while dispersing their investigation'. But the FBI hounds were following several real scents as well as the false one. The Washington Church of Scientology was served with a Grand Jury subpoena for all the personnel records of Michael Meisner on 8 October. They began to burrow and the Grand Jury case dragged on through the winter months. The Guardians several times considered plans to turn Meisner in and hope for a light sentence and an end to the investigation.

During this period Meisner had been moved around motels and lodgings under false names and the strain was beginning to tell. He began to threaten that unless the Wolfe case was settled soon he would surrender. In April 1977, Guardian Henning Heldt issued an order to restrain Meisner and to hold him against his will if he attempted to escape. The Guardians had moved from their role as protectors to one of captors. They had added kidnap to their crimes.

On 1 May, Michael Meisner was told he was to be moved to another apartment. He refused and was bound, gagged and forced into a waiting car and taken to an apartment at 3219 Descanso Drive in Los Angeles and kept there. Eventually in an attempt to relax his captors he agreed to co-operate. His guards were sufficiently relaxed by the end of a month and on 29 May he escaped in a cab and took a Greyhound bus to Las Vegas. From there he telephoned Jim Douglass at the Los Angeles HQ and a meeting was arranged for the next day. The Guardians pressured Meisner to return to Los Angeles and after a meal at Canter's Restaurant he was returned to Descanso Drive.

Meanwhile, the scheduled appearance of agent Silver before the Grand Jury took place on 10 June in Washington, and 'Silvergate' moved into another level of criminality. During cross-examination

Wolfe stated several facts he knew to be false and the following exchange took place:

Q: Now did you know Mr Foster by any other name?
Wolfe: No, I didn't.
Q: You only knew him by John Foster?
Wolfe: Right.

He made these statements when he knew not only the full name and whereabouts of Michael Meisner but who was hiding him.

When the news of Wolfe's Grand Jury appearance crossed to the coast where Meisner was being held, now at an apartment on South Verdugo in Glendale, he made his second attempt to 'blow', this time a successful one. He took two buses to a bowling-alley to evade pursuit and telephoned Assistant Attorney Garey Stark in Washington DC offering to surrender. Within two hours three FBI agents were at the bowling-alley and Meisner was soon on his way to Washington by plane. In order to lull the Guardians into a false sense of security, a letter was dispatched from Meisner (postmarked San Francisco) to Guardian Brian Andrus which stated that he was lying low for a couple of weeks because he needed time to be by himself. The steely response of the top Guardian Mary Sue Hubbard in a communique to Heldt was typical: 'I frankly would not waste Bur I resources looking for him but would instead utilize resources to figure out a way to defuse him should he turn traitor.'

A week after Meisner had surrendered to the authorities, the strike against the Church of Scientology came suddenly and swiftly. At 6 a.m. on 8 July 1977, 134 FBI agents armed with search-warrants and sledgehammers broke into Fifield Manor, the Guardians' HQ in Los Angeles, and simultaneously into the Washington org. Their haul of documents formed the basis of the case which led a Grand Jury on 15 August to indict eleven Guardians — from Mary Sue Hubbard at the top to Sharon Thomas at agent level. Among the eleven were Henning Heldt, Duke Snider and Gerald Bennett Wolfe (alias 'Silver'). But two Guardian chiefs slipped through the net: Jane Kember, Head of the GO Worldwide, and her deputy, Morris ('Mo') Budlong, fled to England.

It took two years to bring the verdict in on the other nine and the sentencing memorandum on the fugitives Kember and Budlong was dated 16 December 1980. During the period between arrest and sentencing, the Scientologists were appealing and wriggling to justify their actions. Kember and Budlong resisted extradition from England

and appealed to the House of Lords. Throughout the process they argued that the Guardians had been tempted into taking their actions because of a long-standing persecution of Scientology by government agencies. Their actions were part of a 'False Report Correction Program' which was to locate false charges against Scientology being held in government files and to eliminate or correct these. Many of these reports, the Church of Scientology contended, were originated by Interpol and spread through its network and unable to be checked or corrected. But the documents seized by the FBI told a very different and sordid story. Many of the documents detailed the special 'drills' used to train a Guardian. 'Intelligence Specialist Training Routine TR-L' trained the student 'how to outflow false data effectively' — in other words, how to lie. The student was supposed to initiate a falsehood upon which he or she would be interrogated. Blinking, looking away when answering or fumbling a response, were all greeted by 'flunk' from the coach and the exercise began over again until 'he/she can lie facilely'. The document gives an example:

Q: Where do you come from?
Student: I come from the Housewives' Committee on Drug Abuse.
Q: But you said earlier that you were single?
Student: Well, actually I was married but I am divorced. I have two kids in the suburbs where I'm a housewife. In fact, I'm a member of the PTA.
Q: What town is that you live in?
Student: West Brighton.
Q: But there is no public school in West Brighton.
Student: I know. I send my children to school in Brighton and that's where I'm a PTA member . . .

Lying was only one of the Guardians' tricks. In a memo of 17 October 1971, Kathy Gregg outlines the twelve steps for a 'strike' ('gathering information on a covert basis'). In May 1974, Deputy Guardian Worldwide, Mo Budlong, had refined this into a manual of 'how a professional operates in stealing materials by infiltration or by straight breaking, entering and theft'. This included how to avoid leaving fingerprints and the use of lock-picking devices. In May 1975, the Guardians were concerned with the difference in law between 'breaking and entering' and 'unlawful entry' and one memo frankly states, 'a large proportion, if not the majority of our high-priority successful collections actions, fall into the category of second-degree burglary, which is a felony'.

While the Guardians claimed that their activities were designed to remove false reports, the documents show otherwise. In a worldwide project dated 16 September 1975, David Gaiman, Deputy Guardian PR W/W, orders the planting of false information in US Security Agency computers 'to hold up American security to ridicule'. The project called for the use of plants to place the information, which would have involved a pedigree cat being placed on record and a sequence of events being planned which would lead to the cat holding a press conference.

The plants in police departments, the IRS, and other government agencies made the Guardians' Office into an amateur espionage agency. Like conventional spies they also developed their escape hatches. 'Project Quaker' dated 9 November 1976 involved setting up a system of safe houses and ready passports so that Guardians wanted by the authorities for questioning could suddenly disappear in such a way that they could not be accused of fleeing prosecution. Since December 1975 there had already been developed an 'early-warning system' using the inside agents to alert the GO to any possible move by the authorities against Scientology and Hubbard in particular. Personal security on Hubbard would then be raised so that he might evade indictment. During the legal process against the eleven GO members, there was a constant fear that Hubbard himself would be implicated. He and his wife Mary Sue separated after the 8 July raid so that he could be distanced from proceedings. In the event, he remained an unindicted co-conspirator.

By far the most sinister and nasty of the GO tricks were practised against those who had been subject to Scientology auditing and whose loyalty to the 'org' had to be ensured. These unsuspecting souls had perhaps imagined that the contents of their 'processing folders' were sacrosanct and (as was taught officially) would in no circumstances be revealed to anyone. They had reckoned without GO 121669 issued by Mary Sue Hubbard on 16 December 1969, which was concerned with the detection of double agents infiltrated into Scientology by the Government or with disaffected Scientologists who might supply information to the authorities. As quoted earlier, it included the following operating targets: 'To make full use of all files on the organization to effect your major target. These include personnel files, Ethics files, dead files, central files, training files, PROCESSING FILES and requests for refunds.' [my caps]. As we have seen, many of the questions asked during auditing touch areas which are intensely personal. 'Engrams', in popular language, might be described as 'hang-ups'. 'Overts' are acts about which one can be expected to feel guilty. Add to these the self-confessed crimes and guilty acts elicited during a 'Sec-Check' and you have the stuff of which emotional blackmail can be made. It was precisely to this area that the Guardians' attention was turned. Michael Meisner was audited sometimes for four hours per day during his eleven months as a fugitive and this information, detailing all his weak points, was found in the documents culled in the raid.

That was just the tip of the iceberg. One file culled in January 1977 from the records of someone who was feeding information about the infiltration used by the GO contains many purple passages. His use of drugs, his *ménage à trois* with his wife and another man in bed together and his forgery of a cheque are all detailed together with his sexual habits and his hang-ups about the size of his penis. His second wife's personal details are then detailed in a separate memo. Both this man (IH) and his wife (K) had given incriminating evidence to the IRS about Scientology and the GO officer summarizing his case concludes: 'This guy sure looks like a plant to me', adding ominously, 'There are a lot of strings to pull on this guy.'

Where no files existed on their enemies, the Guardians would resort to other tricks. Smear-tactics were one of these and there are various drills to help their operatives execute a successful smear. 'Take into account effectiveness, security, legality, workability etc when making your decisions. Choose which basic plan is best', reads the instruction at the head of a sheet in which various scenarios are laid out. Options include calling the enemy's boss and telling him that the man is homosexual, harassing him with threatening phone calls in the middle of the night and spreading false rumours about him. One example concerns a teacher who got a Scientology grant cancelled and is causing trouble for the Church of Scientology. The options for dealing with her are as follows: '(1) Cleverly kidnap her and run reverse processes on her while implanting the phrase "I will never attack Scientology again. I love Scientology." (2) Get copies of the court records where she was found guilty of child-molesting and send a copy to the school principal, Board of Education and a few parents. (3) Send a male PSM in on her who, after she falls in love with him, will get her to move out of the country with him. (4) Pay ten of her students to write dirty phrases about her on the schoolroom blackboard.' These are the only options offered. (Reverse processes are implanting 'engrams' during auditing instead of removing them. It is strictly against the official ethics codes of Scientology and is equivalent to a psychotherapist implanting a neurosis in a patient for spite.)

Other wild schemes involved connecting a bishop opposed to the Church of Scientology to pornographic activities, poisoning a newspaper editor or, more humanely, putting itching powder in his clothes while he is asleep or telling everyone that he is a Communist. It would all be laughable if it were not the case that these very tactics have been used against dozens of people unlucky enough to have acquired the title 'enemy of Scientology'.

In the early 1970s, sociologist Roy Wallis was completing his research project on Scientology eventually published under the title *The Road to Total Freedom* when he became the victim of the Guardians' paranoia. Ironically the book is now accepted by the Public Affairs office of the Church of Scientology as reasonable and fair (they even loaned me a copy) but at the time an undercover agent was sent to Stirling University where Wallis then taught. Posing as a student, he attempted to get Wallis to tell him if he was involved in the drug scene. Wallis recognized him from Saint Hill, so the student then changed his story, claiming to be a defector from the Church of Scientology. In 'The Moral Career of a Research Project' (published within *Doing Sociological Research* in 1977) Wallis describes what happened next: 'In the weeks following his visit a number of forged letters came to light, some of which were supposedly written by me. These letters sent to my university employers, colleagues and others, implicated me in a variety of acts from a homosexual love affair to spying for the drug squad. Because I had few enemies and because this attention followed so closely upon the receipt of my paper by the Church of Scientology organization, it did not seem too difficult to infer the source of these attempts to inconvenience me.'

Writers, journalists, politicians, even judges sitting on cases involving the Church of Scientology — no one was immune from the Guardians. The decade of the seventies had begun with the *Apollo* at sea and Hubbard riding high on the crest of a wave of expansion in orgs around the world. When he came ashore in Clearwater, the boom continued and the Guardians had the confidence to act as if they were an alternative CIA. But by the end of the seventies their crimes were beginning to catch up with them. In December 1979 the nine Guardians received sentences ranging from four to five years and had $10,000 fines imposed. Jane Kember and Mo Budlong were to receive a similar sentence a year later when they were brought back from England to face the music.

It is argued by the Church of Scientology that those responsible for the crimes of the Guardians have been purged from the leadership of the Church of Scientology and the GO has now been abolished. This is perfectly true. Jane Kember ascended the serpentine snake of the Church of Scientology's hierarchy and has descended the ladder of ignominy. She is living in East Grinstead, still a Scientologist but without any position of influence. Mary Sue Hubbard is out of prison and was 'busted' from her posts. On leaving prison, she lived apart from the husband in whose shadow she perpetrated so many of the Guardians' operations. Now a new breed of Young Turks are in charge, but as we shall see, the leopards have not changed their spots.

5 Gamekeepers and Poachers

In the shimmering heat of the Southern Californian desert, a movie crew huddled around their camera. The director was slumped in his canvas-backed chair, his belly bulging out of the trousers held up by a single suspender slung across his shoulder. His long red hair, tinged with grey, was sticking out from under the cowboy hat that shaded his face from the sun. Beside him was a slim youth who was acting as cameraman for the scene which was about to be shot. 'You G-d-d--n, son of bitch,' yelled the director. 'More blood, you f-----g fool! Make it more gory!' Makeup assistant Dell Hartwell, a middle-aged woman who had followed her daughter into Scientology, obliged with more blood from the gallons they had made up by mixing Karo syrup and red food colouring. But it was impossible. The hot sun was drying the glutinous mixture so quickly that the actors' clothes were sticking firmly to their bodies. Once the director had ordered so much that the actors' clothes had literally to be cut off. But you didn't argue with the director. Especially when he was Lafayette Ron Hubbard. They were filming a movie called 'The Unfathomable Man'. It was an appropriate title for Hubbard himself, Mrs Hartwell mused: the founder of a religion who spoke the filthiest language she had heard, and she considered herself broad-minded.

The young cameraman moved quietly about, doing the director's bidding. He had just arrived the month before (in February 1978) and was obviously totally devoted to Ron. He was watching and learning — learning that when Ron wanted something, he shouted. If he didn't get it right away he shouted harder. David Miscavige was barely twenty and was learning by example that if you wanted to get something done you screamed and then it usually *did* get done. He was one of the batch of youngsters from the Commodore's Messenger

Organization who had grown up aboard the *Apollo* and come ashore in Florida. There were others: the young girls who followed Hubbard everywhere, lighting the cigarette that was never out of his hand and even catching the ash when he dropped it.

Hubbard was always dressed in the same outfit — the baggy pants, the cowboy hat and a bandana around his neck — but his clothes were washed and washed and washed again in a special soap. Ron was a stickler for ultra cleanliness and if the set was not clean when he walked on at 8 p.m. then there would be another screaming session.

Day after day they worked on the film, and others, sometimes all through the night with scarcely a break. As often as not the films were never shown. Someone would screw something up and Ron would order the film shelved. Mrs Hartwell and her husband didn't last long. But others did. Miscavige, for instance, who went from strength to strength under the desert sun, as did several of the 'Young Turks' who formed the charmed circle around the leader. Those were energetic times. Hubbard was working hard on developments to the 'tech' of Scientology with David Mayo at his right-hand by day and then turning to the films at night, when Miscavige became the king-pin.

In the autumn of 1978 two big developments took place. The 'New Era Dianetics' breakthrough occurred in September and, a month later, David Mayo was appointed to the newly-created post of Senior Case Supervisor. Mayo was Hubbard's personal auditor from the latter days on the *Apollo* on. Ron once described Mayo as 'the best C/S (case supervisor) in the world.' Eventually Mayo was to suffer a similar fate to McMaster and be expelled ignominiously in the power struggle which was to develop around Hubbard.

The second development in the autumn of 1978 was the purchase of more properties in the area. The film unit had been operating on a 140 acre ranch called Silver and had been using a nearby 10 acre ranch (Monroe) as a studio. Then in October 1978 a former golf and health resort at Gilman Hot Springs was purchased for $2.7 million in cash, along with Massacre Canyon Inn. Gilman was on Route 79, six miles south of Route 10 and about 100 miles south-east of Los Angeles. Hubbard himself lived in nearby Hemet from April 1979 and had a cancer operation on the front of his head shortly after moving there. Kima Douglas, one of his personal physicians, was with him and Mayo arrived to administer 'assists' to the Scientology guru. All mail to the personnel living in these Southern California complexes was channelled through the 'Flag Land Base' at Clearwater, creating a security screen around Hubbard's exact whereabouts. There were then four main centres of Scientology: Saint Hill in Sussex, England, which was barred to Hubbard and other leading Scientologists because of the British Government ban; Clearwater, the Flag Land Base at which many of the higher level courses were available; Los Angeles where the Guardians had their headquarters and where the Church of Scientology had acquired the former Mt. Sinai/Cedars of Lebanon Hospital, a huge blue building at 4833 Fountain Avenue, plus an up-market Celebrity Center to cater for the show-biz personalities who expressed an interest in taking Scientology courses. Finally, there was the enclave in Southern California, the ranches and the houses among which Hubbard moved like a dice beneath a series of upturned cups, it being a matter of guesswork where to find the elusive Commodore of the land-locked fleet.

The security became increasingly necessary as the case against the eleven Guardians was built. In May 1979 the Watchdog Committee was formed with David Miscavige assuming a prominent role despite his tender years and junior rank in the hierarchy of Scientology and the Sea Org. In July, Norman Starkey, a South African who had served his apprenticeship on the *Apollo* in the CMO, announced that the CMO was not a management unit but had the authority to investigate, bypass and 'handle' any area of international management. The Sea Org monsters were beginning to stir and the days of the Guardians were drawing to a close. On 1 September the Watchdog Committee, composed entirely of young CMO types, announced that it had taken over senior management of the church. The power had moved to Southern California and was soon to pass into hidden hands.

In December 1979, the Guardians were sentenced. In January 1980 Ron Hubbard was indicted by the Grand Jury in Tampa, Florida, and other indictments were pending elsewhere throughout the United States, including a lawsuit by a former CMO member, Tonja, who alleged she had been made into Hubbard's serf. The escape plan was sprung. Hubbard hurriedly left Hemet with Pat and Annie Broeker to begin his life as a recluse. Officially the news was that he had gone away to write the sequel to the magnum opus *Battlefield Earth*, which was already on its way to the publishers and would revive his career as a science-fiction writer. Behind the scenes it was perfectly clear that Hubbard was fleeing the courts and what they could do to him in the wake of the revelations from the Guardians' Office documents.

Two other matters were on Hubbard's mind — money and mortality. He was approaching the lifespan of three score years and ten and had not been in the best of health in the late seventies. 'Dropping the body' — in org-speak a term for death — might not be far away. Taking the tenets of Scientology at their face value, this would entail coming back again in a future life and thus it was logical that Hubbard would want to enjoy a leading role within the organization he had founded when he came back from the dead. A giant among thetans could not be expected to work his way up, so there were to be trust funds set up so that Ron could again inherit his kingdom. His treasure on earth was assessed according to the use which the Church of Scientology had made of trademarks, copyrights and so forth. Remember that every little piece of paper which became a HCOB, every taped lecture, every slogan across the wall of an org building, all had the tiny subscript 'Copyright L. Ron Hubbard'. Ron was owed a lot: $85 million was the agreed sum.

It is not easy to untangle the web of Church of Scientology finances. Scientology is a multi-national company for some purposes and just as opaque as any multi-national corporation to any prying eye which wishes to view a balance-sheet. It is in many countries a tax-exempt charity. Its personnel work for little or no reward and are required to maintain secrecy about org finances. Thus in the USA the IRS are extremely interested in finding out anything they can about Scientology finances and since they are one of the principal perceived enemies of Scientology every effort is made to thwart them.

The IRS hunted Scientology thoughout the seventies with the Church of Scientology proving as wily as a fox in shifting its millions around and having as many lairs.

The IRS had claimed as far back as 1972 that the Church of Scientology owed it $1 million in taxes for the years 1970–72. But testimony given in the Armstrong case in 1984 indicated that the real figure was much higher than this. In the years 1970–82 it was revealed that Hubbard had secretly diverted more than $100 million from the church into foreign bank-accounts which he controlled. Although he had supposedly cut his ties with the church on coming ashore in the mid-seventies, and received only a token consulting fee of $35,000 annually, he had actually been using 'shell' corporations to channel money to his overseas accounts. Laurel Sullivan left the Church of Scientology in 1981 after serving fifteen years, the last eight as Hubbard's personal public relations adviser. She admitted that from 1972–81 she was in charge of a secret operation to transfer money from church funds to Hubbard through a 'corporate shell', the Religious Research Foundation (RRF), incorporated in Liberia with accounts in banks in Lichtenstein and Luxemburg. When she left Scientology in 1981, said Mrs Sullivan, RRF's assets were between $200 million and $300 million, and at one point in the 1970s they totalled $330 million.

Kima Douglas, Hubbard's personal medical officer until she left Scientology in 1980, testified that she had helped establish fourteen or fifteen foundations, including the RRF, and had couriered 'hundreds of thousands of dollars out of the United States' in violation of Federal laws requiring cash amounts of over $5,000 to be disclosed to customs officials.

Hubbard's philosophy on money was defined by him in Policy Letters of 27 November and 3 December 1971. Exhorting his orgs to do better and make bigger profits, Hubbard wrote: 'Basically *money* is an idea backed by confidence . . . remember, *money* represents *things*. It is a substitute for goods and services. What governments, people and even our orgs can't get understood is that NO PRODUCTION = No Money . . . as it exists at this writing; the only real crime in the West is for a group to be without money. That finishes it. But with enough money it can defend itself and expand. Yet if you borrow money you become the property of bankers. If you make money you become the target of tax collectors.'

As is clear fom his writings elsewhere, Hubbard was paranoiac about both bankers and the taxmen of the IRS.

Because the Church of Scientology does not publish accounts and does not officially acknowledge those foreign accounts which are 'Mr Hubbard's private affair', it is impossible to tell how much is still in them. But one thing is certain. Church income and assets had fallen drastically by the time Hubbard disappeared in 1980. The bad publicity generated by the trial of the Guardians' Office eleven had been felt through a chilly downdraught in statistics. There was a heavy run of demands for refunds at Saint Hill. The Guardians' Office itself was in disarray and the only option facing the Church of Scientology was to close it down and announce that it had chopped off the rotten branch. But it was the roots of Scientology that were feeling the drought of money. Back in 1964 Hubbard had decreed that 25 hours of auditing should equal three months' wages. This was subsequently reduced in 1965 because it was found to be too pricey. 250 hours of auditing to go 'Clear' was considered a minimum and that meant nearly three years' wages. So prices were trimmed back. But the temptation to squeeze captive customers was too great when the financial drought hit the orgs. Based on a formula outlined by Hubbard, an 'intensive' session would cost half a month's wages. On several occasions between 1980 and 1982 an 'intensive' was costing as much as twice the monthly average wage in the USA. The immediate effect of this was felt in the Missions, franchise operations run on Scientology lines. The church was not responsible for their running costs, but the Mission holders were Scientologists who paid 10% of their income to the Church of Scientology. Their other main function was to create 'Clears'. Since the Missions were not allowed to give advanced courses they were required to push their Clears on to take further courses, or 'flow them up the Bridge' in org-speak. A drop in Mission income meant a double penalty on the church — loss of franchise income and loss of raw material from which the cream of their fees would come. Thus the scene was set for the first major development: a conference at which the Mission holders could be galvanized into action.[1]

What that action should be was not at all evident as Hubbard had ceased to be in regular communication with other parts of the organization. His communication lines were controlled by the Broekers who were with him in hiding and by David Miscavige who set up a unit in early 1981 known as the All Clear Unit, which was allegedly designed to work towards a situation when Hubbard 'could come back on lines', i.e., resume a high profile. He never did. It was the All Clear Unit instead which became all-powerful. In 1981 David Miscavige had begun the year as a cameraman at Gilman Hot Springs and a junior member of the Commodore's Messenger Organization. He ended it in charge of the Watchdog Committee and the All Clear Unit which he announced was now senior to CMO International. Because the actions of these committees were assumed to have the sanction of Hubbard himself, the rapid rise to power of this twenty-three-year-old was not questioned. But once he had assumed power the new supremo had to consolidate his position. Here is how he did it:

When the All Clear Unit was set up in early 1981, there were thirty-five liability suits against the Church of Scientology naming Hubbard. The Unit was small, consisting of Miscavige, Diane Voegerding, Lois Riesdorf, Gale Irwin, Norman Starkey and Terri Gamboa. Of these, Miscavige, Gale Irwin and Lois Riesdorf were also key figures in the Watchdog Committee, which included additionally Marc Yaeger, John Nelson and Diane Voegerding (the CO CMO). On 27 June, Voegerding was handed a dispatch from Miscavige requesting her to stand down as CO CMO. She complied and was replaced by her

[1] see page 99

sister, Gale Irwin. Then on 1 July, Miscavige called on Mary Sue Hubbard with a letter prepared by lawyers which argued that MSH's presence as the Guardians' controller implicated Hubbard in all church matters including the GO cases. She stepped down and was later removed from office, as was Jane Kember.

On 5 August 1981, a Comm Ev was convened on several leading GO officials including David Gaiman, Duke Snider, Mo Budlong and Henning Heldt. The six-strong Committee included Miscavige, Yaeger and Nelson. They were all found guilty and deposed. In September, Miscavige showed an order to Gale Irwin stating that the All Clear Unit was no longer junior to CO CMO. In December, Gale Irwin was replaced as CO CMO by John Nelson, for allegedly falsifying data sent to Hubbard in November. Having put a dozen eggs in his two baskets of All Clear and Watchdog, Miscavige was now reducing them to half a dozen eggs in one basket. That one key basket was to be the Religious Technology Center (RTC).

The RTC was to be a non-profit-making corporation based at 6517 Sunset Boulevard, Los Angeles. Its initial trustees were David Miscavige, David Mayo, Terri Gamboa, Lyman Spurlock, Norman Starkey, Julia Watson and Phoebe Maurer. Of these key figures, Watson, Gamboa, Spurlock, Starkey and, of course, Miscavige, were no longer on the Scientology staff. Amazingly, Miscavige had resigned his church contracts in early 1982 and had gone to head an organization called Author Services Incorporated (ASI). This was a Los Angeles based PROFIT-MAKING corporation administering the income from Hubbard's prodigious writings, both fiction and non-fiction, and acting in tandem with Bridge Publications. The anomaly was that the RTC was now to be the bastion of orthodoxy within Scientology, overseeing the 'tech' with full rights to all Hubbard's works, yet its trustees were not senior officials of the church they controlled. They were not accountable to anyone save themselves.

The most sensational fact about the RTC was not who was in it, but the document which set it up. One of the stated purposes of the RTC was to get Hubbard off the hook of legal action by individuals or the authorities. In return for the use of the trademarks and rights to the Scientology materials, the document setting up RTC, dated 16 May 1982, declares: 'RTC hereby indemnifies LRH and agrees to hold him harmless from and against all liabilities, claims and actions of any kind, and costs, including attorney's fees, which relate to the Marks or services in connection with which they are used.' This seems to put quite a large distance between Hubbard and the Church of Scientology and, indeed, the articles of the RTC were produced in a lawsuit in Omaha to make this very point. However, what the RTC did not produce was Section 4 of the original document setting up the RTC, which granted an option to the Church of Spiritual Technology (CST) to purchase back all the trademarks and rights for the sum of $100 if it was not satisfied with the situation as managed by the RTC, and the CST (a Hubbard front) would have sole discretion and judgment in this regard. Section 4 had been omitted from the court submission. But that was the least of the omissions. The documents submitted to the court did not include the seal of the Notary Public who had supervised the RTC articles. Examination of a photocopy of the original which I have in my possession shows the Notary Public to be none other than one DAVID MISCAVIGE! The RTC documents were apparently signed on 10 May 1982 before Miscavige in the County of Los Angeles by L. Ron Hubbard. A further agreement between Hubbard and the RTC was signed on 15 June 1982 with Miscavige as Notary.

Both of Hubbard's signatures on these documents have been pronounced forgeries by handwriting experts. Irmgard Wassard, a Danish graphologist, declared: 'There is a probability amounting almost to certainty (a) that the two signatures have been made by the same person and (b) that that person is *not* identical with the person (L. Ron Hubbard) . . . since the doubtful signatures show a multitude of deviations from the authentic writing which are typical of forgeries.' A further opinion from another leading expert graphologist, John J. Swanson, stated: 'Using the L. Ron Hubbard signatures in Exhibit 3 as standard and the basis for comparison, it is the opinion of the examiner that the L. Ron Hubbard signatures in Exhibits 1 and 2 are not the same and were not written by the individual represented by the signatures in Exhibit 3.' *(See Appendix B.)*

In April 1984 former senior Church of Scientology official Diane Voegeding, signed an affidavit to the effect that between March 1980 and December 1981 David Miscavige did not see Hubbard but had a page of signatures in his Notary Book which he could assign to documents without Hubbard appearing before him. Since he no longer met Hubbard personally, Miscavige gave the book to Pat Broeker who would return it within a week with a page of LRH signatures entered. This procedure, Voegeding attested, had been followed through to the first months of 1983. Thus whether it was a case of forged signatures or 'blind' signatures, it would appear that it was not Hubbard who was underwriting the activities of the Broekers, Miscavige and the RTC. They were their own masters.

It must be said that in support of the bona fides of the signatures is the Probate document of 15 May, which was accepted by the court as genuinely signed by Hubbard *(see Appendix C)*. In it he says: 'I have transferred my religious trademarks to the Religious Technology Center, but I retain full ownership of any commercial application of the marks as well as full ownership of all my copyrights and patent rights, none of which have been transferred. Contrary to the uninformed allegations of the petition, my trademark transfer involved no monetary loss. Finally, I and only I sign my name on any of my accounts or contract documents, etc. There is no truth to the allegation that anyone else signs my checks or other financial documents using my name.'

So what are we to believe? Was the RTC set up invalidly in 1982 but subsequently endorsed by Hubbard? Was the 'fudging' of who owned the trademarks after 1982 a joint ploy by the RTC and Hubbard, or had his disciples duped Hubbard into thinking he still had control? Could the disputed signatures have been executed by someone incapacitated by a stroke? Was he perhaps totally incapacitated during the years 1982–6, or, as some still believe, already dead — and the RTC acting on his behalf? Whatever the truth, the issue is now closed since in his will Hubbard left control of Scientology to the RTC anyway.

One decision which Hubbard can be assumed to have made personally was the appointment of David Mayo in April 1982 to take over the supervision of the 'tech'. He was to be the arbiter of orthodoxy and was given this responsibility for 20–25 years in a letter. The reason we can conclude that this was genuine was that Mayo was not approved of by the new cabal. His days were numbered and they were later to deny that any such communication existed. Back in November 1981 Mayo had been asked by Hubbard to 'Sec-Check' Pat Broeker. Presumably the Scientology supremo LRH wanted his sole line of communication to the outside world to be a safe one. However, the Mayo report was not entirely favourable and Broeker is accused by Mayo of having altered it and retyped it to his satisfaction. Mayo found out and complained about the lies on LRH's 'comm lines'. There followed a rumour that Mayo was plotting a takeover. This was a sure method of firing the paranoia of Hubbard when the rumour came boomeranging back to him. From that moment on, there was no one who could prevent the toppling of Mayo from power.

The move came in October 1982, six months after Mayo's elevation. He was Comm Eved along with several other senior figures whose experience of 'Standard Tech' made them threats to the new guard.

These were known as the Happy Valley Comm Evs and they effectively stilled the voices of authority who might have challenged what was being done by Miscavige and Co in the name of 'helping Ron'. (Mayo alleges that Miscavige told him that he was going to 'break him'.)

Happy Valley was far from living up to its name. It was a box canyon in the Palm Springs area surrounded by an Indian reservation on which the Church of Scientology owned a ranch. Mayo and his staff of five plus another eleven people were put on a running programme which Hubbard had developed along with the Purification Rundown to attain physical fitness. It was meant to be on a gradient with more exercise each day, but the way the programme was inflicted on Mayo and the others, Happy Valley resembled a convict camp with hard labour thrown in. In the desert heat the inmates would be required to undertake gruelling runs for up to twelve hours per day. Mayo recounts how he would sit down and the supervisor would walk towards him shouting but he would resume running just before he arrived, and simultaneously the other group would sit down, causing the guard to have to run to and fro to bully them into action. They kept up this taunting and teasing throughout their captivity.

Mayo was eventually liberated in February of the following year (1983) and declared a SP. He formed an Advanced Ability Center where he taught his own version of the 'tech' and upper thetan levels. This meant he was subject to legal and personal harassment by the Church of Scientology for using its materials. He counter-sued for an injunction to stop this and became a focus for many of the Scientologists who were still loyal to Hubbard's tech but who had left the church or were expelled in the turmoil of the years 1982–4. Mayo remains loyal to Scientology, convinced that Hubbard would not have sanctioned his demotion if he had not been fed false rumours by the Miscavige cabal.

Around the time the RTC was set up, Miscavige ordered a visible symbol of the new era to be built at the new and unofficial 'Flag' HQ in Southern California. It was a full-sized replica clipper-ship complete with sails and masts, embedded in the ground at Gilman Springs and surrounded by palm trees and a swimming-pool. The cost was $565,000 and the labour was supplied by the Sea Org, who, it has to be said, have made a magnificent job of finishing the ship.

To take a further grip on the finances of Scientology, in June 1982 the Watchdog Committee set up an organization to be known as the International Finance Police. One cannot but have sympathy with the bewildered IRS officials who were berated by the Church of Scientology for persecuting a religion and who were then confronted with this 'religion' setting up Finance Police. The overlord of Scientology's money was Wendell Reynolds who was given the title 'Dictator'. It was no joke. The IFP were determined to put the squeeze on the Missions. But to launch this blitzkrieg, Miscavige orchestrated a meeting in San Francisco for 17 October which was to prove momentous in the history of Scientology. It was the 1982 Mission Holders' Conference, referred to earlier.

The transcript of that meeting makes interesting reading. Even more interesting are the differences between the official transcript circulated to the orgs after the conference and the actual words spoken. The meeting opened with a softening-up session explaining the new structure with the RTC as top dog and went on to deal with the dangerous heresies ('out-tech' and 'squirrelling') which were creeping in and had to be eradicated. In brutal manner the Mission holders were told by a succession of RTC speakers, including Miscavige, that if they didn't do what they were told then they would be expelled, forbidden to use Scientology, declared Suppressive, even jailed. Verbal abuse, flash-bulbing (intimidation by photographing a person repeatedly with flash), threats, humiliation — it's all there. Here are a few choice extracts:

> **LARRY HELLER** (*Church of Scientology attorney*): My law firm has been instructed to make sure that if there is in fact an unauthorized use of any of these trademarks, if it is determined that the mark was not used in accordance with source that we enforce the RTC's rights which I've just described to you throughout the judicial procedure to get a superior court of US Court judgment and then enforce that judgment through contempt and criminal proceedings.

> **Commander DAVID MISCAVIGE**: Earlier this evening both Kingsley Wimbush and Dean Stokes were here. They have both now been declared and we are pursuing criminal charges against them. They have been delivering their own squirrel tech while calling it Scientology. Kingsley Wimbush's 'dinging process' is complete squirrel. You won't find it in any tech, yet he has been calling it Scientology. That's a violation of trademark laws and he now faces some serious charges for this crime. This sort of activity is NOT going to go on any more. [At this point Wimbush's wife who was unaware that he had been 'bounced' on his way to the

meeting, got up to leave and the tape of the proceedings records Miscavige hissing, 'Declare her!']

Commander STEVE MARLOWE *(Inspector General from the RTC)*: The fact of the matter is that you have a new breed of management in the church. They're tough. They're ruthless. They are 'on source'. They don't get muscled around by crazy loonies, they don't get muscled around by people who are squirrelling, none of that. On this team you're playing with the winning team, totally and utterly.

Commander NORMAN STARKEY *(of a defector)*: Where is he now? He was working for Flynn! He will never, never, I promise you, for any life-time get any auditing or ever have a chance to get out of his trap. And those of you who are on OT III know what that means. That means dying and dying and dying and dying again. Forever, for eternity . . . we will take action in the defence of our religion. If anybody's going to try to stop that and if I didn't stop them from trying to stop it, it would be an overt that I would be committing.

Commander RAY MITHOFF: For someone who's out there squirrelling and trying to get other people's attention off Scientology, just to fatten their own pocket or whatever. That person's future is black . . . I can't even find the words to describe how black that person's future is. In fact, it is almost as black as the future of an FBI agent.

Commander/Dictator **WENDELL REYNOLDS** then mounted the rostrum and made the audience there and then write down all their O/Ws (overts and withholds, or sins to use religious terminology). 'If you don't come clean and I find out something later on, that P/L is enforced. You are guilty of anything you didn't report on. Right per that P/L. We talk the same language?'

The purpose of the meeting was (1) to force the Missions to accept the new RTC structure; (2) to frighten potential 'squirrels' into conformity; (3) to stress that all Missions must make sure their clients were 'flowed up the Bridge' and that they met higher statistical targets. To achieve this last aim, targets were imposed there and then. But in the opening address when the Church of Scientology attorney Larry Heller was speaking, significant changes were made in the transcript later circulated to the orgs. I have bracketed in caps after the 'official' version the words actually used:

'All of the Scientology/Dianetic trademarks were previously owned (ARE OWNED IN PERPETUITY) by L. Ron Hubbard (who) has donated (LICENSED) the vast majority of those to a corporation which some of you have probably heard of, by the name of the Religious Technology Center.'

Quite apart from the subtle dishonesty in the transcript which hid the cosmetic Clause 4 of the RTC's articles of incorporation, the RTC continued to present the façade (to outsiders) that Hubbard had retired from the scene, whereas among its own members it suggested that Hubbard still had his finger on the pulse. The overall effect was to portray the RTC as the reigning sole authority on the 'tech'. It is also salutary that throughout the whole transcript there is scarcely a mention of Hubbard by name or by quotation, which is unusual for any Scientology gathering, which normally oozes obeisance to LRH.

Following the Mission Holders' Conference in 1982, there was intense activity by the Finance Police. They were descending on Missions demanding their $15,000 per day consultation fee and squeezing them for more money. Reserves were siphoned off. When Bent Corydon returned to his Riverside mission his $2 million reserves had vanished. Another $2 million was raised in increased revenue in the wake of the Hilton Hotel meeting. But Miscavige was in danger of killing the geese which were laying his golden eggs. Twenty-five of the ninety-eight Missions in the US network defected or were bankrupted and closed their doors. The RTC cleaned out the bank accounts. But this growing number of defectors, declared Suppressives and deposed senior executives were still loyal to 'Ron'. They still believed in the 'tech' as they had been taught it and had passed it on to others. Most of them had joined Scientology for its declared purpose of 'clearing the planet' and their zeal was looking for an outlet. They were soon joined by many Scientologists from within the Church of Scientology who had begun to realize that all was not well with the new leadership. One of the significant catalysts for defections was the 'Dane Tops letter'. This pseudonymous and lengthy circular questioned whether all that was being done by the RTC was in line with 'Standard Tech'. It was plausible and reasonable, and appealed to many more discerning Scientologists who might have toed the RTC line but were dismayed by the bully-boy tactics of the new leadership. The trickle of defections became a flood. The Church of Scientology responded by 'declaring' those who were challenging its leadership. Many of them were the more qualified auditors and when the dust had settled, it was evident that the turmoil of 1982 was not merely some letting of bad blood within the organization but the transfusion of some of its lifeblood into a new body, an independent Church of Scientology.

Of course, the new movement could not use the name Scientology. Advanced Ability Centers were set up on the doorstep of the orgs and much of the bitterness which is found among religious sectarianism was evident. The independents lowered their prices and threatened to undercut the RTC controlled Church of Scientology, which responded with lawsuits and a vitriolic propaganda newsletter entitled *Stamp out Squirrels*. In England, many of the independents opened up on the doorstep of Saint Hill in East Grinstead where they already lived.

A young businessman Scientologist, Jon Atack, started the newsletter *Reconnection*, which provided a communication network for the lost souls who had spent possibly most of their adult lives within Scientology and at the age of thirty had been declared Suppressives and therefore lost in one blow their friends, their job and their religion. At first they were confused, even bitter, then determined to build a better org to replace the old. Perhaps as they built up contacts and settled in the social world outside Scientology, they began to consider turning their back on the whole business of Dianetics and Scientology. Robin Scott, who opened his centre at Candacraig, followed such a path. Jon Atack began by hating the anti-Scientology lawyer Michael Flynn just as vehemently as he did Miscavige and Co. but gradually he came to accept that Flynn was well-motivated and justified in his campaign.

Perhaps this withdrawal process is a lengthy but necessary antidote to the long indoctrination sequence into the Church of Scientology which DeWolf described as 'brain-washing spread over a lifetime'. Perhaps the independents will manage to establish their 'orgs' as a vitiated version of Scientology. My own view is that they will not. Partly because the tide of bad publicity, lawsuits and financial exposure that is growing in intensity with each ebb and flow will engulf the official church and the independents and will sweep away any support they might gather from the general public. Partly because the psychological 'winding down' process which I have just described will have the effect of gradually deprogramming them. They will drift away from involvement, particularly after they are free for any length of time from the regimented constraints of Sea Org discipline. But most of all, because of Flynn's argument that Scientology 'begins and ends in the mindset of L. Ron Hubbard'. Any structure built on this foundation is built on the shifting sands of paranoia and power mania which will not withstand the tide of public opinion.

The Church of Scientology has effected several changes in its public relations since the purges. These are represented to the outsider as cleansing the stables, not only purging the Guardians but expelling Mission holders who were ripping off the orgs. When the *Sunday Times* magazine published accounts of the Happy Valley Comm Evs in a long feature in November 1984, Michael Garside, the Public Affairs Director at Saint Hill, wrote: 'Following a "house-cleaning" by the church in 1981–83 some members were expelled for misconduct, some others left with them. A few attempts were made by some of these to establish independent Scientology counselling organizations outside the church but these have by and large foundered. Several key-figures in this movement have publicly attacked the church but evidence of criminal activity against the church by some of these individuals greatly lessens their credibility.' He went on to cite Robin Scott and Bent Corydon as two figures who had received sentences in court.

The official church is insistent that the RTC is a background body of trustees, that Miscavige is a minor figure, that stats are high and that everything in the garden is rosy. Scientologists are anxious to welcome visitors to Saint Hill — particularly Members of Parliament — to improve the church's public relations image. The same is true of other centres. When I visited Los Angeles, the two guardian angels from the Scientology PR Department who conducted me round, Susan Jones and Shirley Young, were not Guardians in the bad old sense of the seventies, but courteous and willing guides to the complex of buildings around Los Angeles. It is sometimes argued that the Church of Scientology is extra careful to be nice to celebrities and rich clients, who are not subjected to the strict discipline, low pay and punishment of the ordinary staff member. I cannot deny that I, as a writer, was very well treated, and I am sure my guides did not lie — but neither do the documents which have come into my possession since that visit.

As I walked round the room where E-Meters are assembled within the huge blue Cedars of Lebanon complex which used to be a hospital, I asked questions which were answered in very technical terms. Notices proclaimed this to be a 'high security area'. The Advanced Org for Los Angeles (AULA) is in a separate part of the building and bears a notice 'Never leave a briefcase unlocked when not in a locked cabinet'. A more relaxed atmosphere pervades the other parts of the building. But everywhere there are pictures of Hubbard and in every building in the Los Angeles complex there is an 'LRH' office. This shrine was for Ron's use 'should he come back and want it'. Usually there are a few mementoes of the *Apollo* days and a few familiar 'LRH' photographs. It is a shade eerie and perhaps even a shade ridiculous since Ron showed no inclination whatsoever of coming anywhere near these vast properties acquired by the Church of Scientology.

At 5930 Franklin Avenue is the Celebrity Center which used to be a hotel used by many movie stars, when it was called Château Élycée. 'We don't use that name because some dictionaries define it as "the house of the dead" — and we're very much alive,' smiled my guide. The mini-hall of fame includes such personalities as Chick Corea the jazz pianist; Karen Black; Cathy Lee Crosby; Stanley Clarke; John Travolta and Priscilla Presley (who was lying on her side in portrait form opposite a gaudy portrait of her famous husband). 'This is the place for the aesthetic types rather than the rich,' declared Irish New Yorker Pat who runs the place. 'The artist and the dreamer have a haven here where they're in a safe environment. They can see their own peers.'

In 1981 the Celebrity Center gobbled up the Fifield Manor building which since the demise of the Guardians really was a château of the dead. It was the brain-child of the late Yvonne Jentzsch who was apparently a gentle but charismatic personality who charmed many stars to enter Scientology's portals. Apart from Ron, she was the only person to have the distinction of a shrine/office to herself in any Church of Scientology org. Her husband, Heber Jentzsch, a former actor, was appointed by the RTC to be titular President of the Church of Scientology and I was scheduled to meet him over lunch.

Heber Jentzsch is tall, in his early forties, with glasses and greying hair. His handshake is firm and he is larger than life. Born a Mormon in Utah, he was out playing in the fields after a nearby A-bomb test when it rained and the radiation burns on his skin nearly killed him. When he tells the story you can see the rain, the hills, the scars. He is a born preacher and swashbuckles into attacks on arch-enemies attorney Flynn and psychiatrist John Clark and the dreaded IRS as we talk. We are facing the clash of two cultures, he rages. The persecution of religion by the Gestapo of the IRS. No, he is not worried about spending millions on lawsuits. These are the price of freedom. But he is optimistic. 'The enemy can't keep up their hate-mongering year after year without the spring recoiling.' How did I get on with Flynn, he asks. When I tell him that I have visited the Boston attorney's office and render the questions Michael Flynn told me to put to him in a passable imitation of Flynn's 'Boston Irish' voice, Heber roars with laughter. He tells me that he has a little surprise for me that afternoon. I had asked to see the Gilman Springs property. Well, he would drive me there. It was an offer I could not refuse.

As we drove down Highway 79 the hundred miles or so to Gilman, Heber talked expansively about the issues facing the Church of Scientology. Critics say he is an actor who is no more than a PR front since the Presidency carries no real power, but he is the official voice and so I switched on my tape recorder with his permission as we drove down past the date-palms towards the desert area of Palm Springs. These are extracts from that conversation:

SL: You knew Hubbard well personally?

HJ: No, I never met Mr Hubbard. My first wife before she passed away, worked extensively with Mr Hubbard and I've written to Mr Hubbard extensive correspondence and my wife Karen, whom you've met, worked extensively with Mr Hubbard; a number of people have. I feel there is a friendship there, obviously. I feel . . . I feel like every other Scientologist, . . . I know the man through his works. Can one love Shakespeare without having met the man?

SL: Yes.

HJ: Can one appreciate Shelley, Keats, Poe, and others without having met the man? Absolutely. There is another force of work there and that's the force that Flynn cannot deal with because that force is the work itself. The communication of a man and self. To bring it all down to one infinitesimal 'Did-he-graduate-from-George-Washington-University?' argument, is incredible. He's also said, you know, he's not a doctor, he doesn't have a doctor's degree. Well, fine. Dr Mengele had a nice doctor's degree and look what he did. Well, let's go the other round, Alexander Graham Bell didn't have a degree so shall we throw away all the telephones and all the communications systems we have in the world today because he didn't have a doctor's degree? Give me a break. Or let's take Thomas Eddison . . . .

SL: But you must be as curious as anybody, you must be more curious than I am, to see, to meet, to hear Ron Hubbard speak?

HJ: . . . Sure I'd like to see that, I would, you know . . . . there's a greater . . . greater point there. I can appreciate more than people can know his right to privacy and if that man chose to be a private person for the rest of his life, which I don't think he could do . . . . Well, you know, I've been asked that before. It's a good question. You've got to understand Hubbard. He doesn't care whether people have that concept, he's more interested in mankind itself than the potential interpretation of him. . . .

SL: Curiosity, though, begs me to ask the next question. Who does see him now?

HJ: . . . Well, of course . . . Hubbard has always had periods of his life where he's just taken off and he's a very private person . . . .

SL: Sure, very private, and I would think if you've got an organization around you like that, it's possible you could become drugged by it and get high on the ego trip. Or, on the other hand, you could react against it and want to go away and get away from it. Do you ever wonder if you'll meet him out driving one day or suddenly you'll be . . .

HJ: You wonder, yes . . . I used to a lot but I don't put a lot of attention on it nowadays. It is kind of like . . .

SL: Because you're too busy . . . ?

HJ: But also it's kind of like Hubbard knows where we are. I don't have to know where he is. In other words, it's a church's role to establish a bulkhead, a visible, physical organization or established units.

SL: Some journalistic accounts that I've seen have suggested that — I think *Time Magazine* was one of the first to sort of hint at it — that . . . Miscavige . . . and his Young Turks had taken over . . .

HJ: Oh yeah, the Young Turks they call them . . .

SL: And they are running the organization, or an alternative explanation is that they're running the organization on instructions from Hubbard . . .

HJ: Yeah, they use both of those . . .

SL: Now you can't have both of those.

HJ: You can't have it both ways . . . Miscavige doesn't run Scientology and I know him, he was aboard the ship, my wife knew him. He has worked with Hubbard directly on filming and stuff like that . . . . technician capability and so forth, and, you know, it's like . . . I get all these allegations, I love it in a way. Do you know what they're saying? Do you realize that the magnitude . . . Flynn says this over and over again. He's just a kid who's 25 years of age, and is capable of running 600 organizations singlehandedly . . . You show me any church or any major . . . corporation . . . where one individual can run it all.

SL: Why does David Miscavige get such a prominent place, though, if he just makes films now?

HJ: Well he's done films and stuff like that. Why does he get a prominent place like that?

SL: Yes. Now why do these people make that accusation?

HJ: I think that the people who were thrown out have had a personal vendetta against him and would do anything possible to try to get back at him and if government is the vehicle or Press is the vehicle, because they all mention it, or if they felt that in any way that someone . . . You have to go back to the clash of two ideas and you'd be in Clark's paper. He said in order to knock out the cults — I'm paraphrasing, I'll give you the exact quote when I get it for you — in order to knock out the cults, says he, knock out the core group, knock out the leaders. Why? Clash of two ideas. Why would you want to do that to a religion? Anyway, those arguments as to who was with Mr Hubbard, very honestly, I don't know . . . .

SL: How do the directives come, then, because a lot of people from the outside would see you, because you're President, as the sort of titular head.

HJ: I receive and the Board receives Policy Letters which are written by Mr Hubbard and . . .

SL: In his own handwriting?

HJ: Sometimes in his own handwriting, sometimes they're typed. These are then sent to the Board for approval. They are approved by the Board and then they go to general distribution or whatever distribution is general throughout the world. Hubbard has always maintained that . . . See, here's the interesting thing. They keep saying that Hubbard is running, Hubbard is controlling, Hubbard is doing it all. All right, whatever . . . the point that's interesting in all that is that Hubbard for years and years, even in the very beginning, he never wanted to establish organizations. He never wanted to have to run organizations. He never wanted to have to develop entire technologies for the people and so forth. He never wanted to have to train people on how to audit and so forth . . . . and you'll see him lamenting the fact that he's pulled back into the organization but that's precisely why, and this is hard for people to understand, Hubbard's not interested in power. He gives it to you as an individual in your own life. And so he says OK here, you're the one with all the capabilities, use them, go ahead.

SL: You mentioned earlier Gerry Armstrong as being your stepson and that obviously must be a bitter thing to witness, the sense that he has become one of the great enemies of the Church of Scientology.

HJ: There's no path in life that one walks that there isn't some difficulties.

SL: Why did he turn like that?

HJ: Well, I think there was a . . . a kind of resentment that was unexpressed for a long time with Gerry. Finally he expressed it. His research is . . . well, let's look at it this way. For example, he says . . . Mr Hubbard was never a commander on a ship. So we go and we dig up all of these records and so forth and so on. Well, Gerry, what did you do? — 'Well, I checked several books. Well, I can read several books and then end my search, can I not?'

You're a reporter, you can say well that's books on naval history and you didn't see Ron Hubbard mentioned so I guess that's it.

Well, wait a minute, you say, all right, fine — what if I analyze a little further. Did he or did he not? Why didn't you go to naval archives in Washington DC? 'Well I just didn't.' Well, here are the documents on Mr Hubbard which show that he was involved in action. How do you respond to that? 'Well, I guess I stand corrected.'

SL: And that's in the record is it?

HJ: That's in the record. So, all right, you stand corrected. Well, that's great. You know, it's like a guy just walked in there, threw a bunch of bombs around the place, shattered up the whole walls and so forth, caused hopefully, he thinks, a lot of damage. You confront him with it and he says — 'Oh yeah, well, I guess', and you say that your motivation . . . you thought that people who lived there should have been destroyed. Now that you've found out that they weren't what you thought they were, how do you feel about that? By golly, I mean look at this information, how do you feel? 'You know, I stand corrected.' But some people were injured. 'Well, I guess I was acting on the best information I had — well, it doesn't work that way.' That's Gerry. I think his problem was and is that he's deeply disturbed by competence and Hubbard . . . represents competence, and so do other people. So one can have criminal competence or one can have religious competence or one can have professional competence or whatever. Competence can be in any one of those fields. It is the intention with which one is working that's important and what is produced. . . .

SL: What do you think the future will be? How will the church evolve? I mean, Ron's not going to live forever.

HJ: There's a lot of his enemies would hope that. Well, I've been asked that question I think maybe once or twice and I have my own personal perceptions which I probably won't go into . . . . First of all, Mr Hubbard has taken very good care of himself. He's also worked extremely hard and he's brung that body through a lot of strenuous moments . . . I come from Utah: friends of mine there, gentlemen of my city and farming town — 104, 105, 107 they live to be. Now I would hope Mr Hubbard would be sticking around for the next thirty years just to outlive every one of his enemies. Well, by that time . . . I think the real question that's being asked is this. What's the growth rate going to be while he is still around? We do greatly appreciate and love this man. It isn't that we have to do something for Mr Hubbard, we have to do something for ourselves, that's what Scientology is — and as a group. Of course our concept is that we're not just a faith system, it is of the soul in terms. That's hard to understand in Western civilization but completely comprehensible in Eastern civilization and accepted without too much of a problem. So I would say that Mr Hubbard's going to be around for a good deal longer and if and when he does decide to leave and return, then I think the return is as important as the . . . more important than the leaving. I think it'll be for a very short duration and the church will be developed, capable, stabilized to such a point that there's no problem. See you have to kind of look at movements historically — Buddha — his life was ended because one of his disciples . . . poisoned him. Well, look what Buddha did in that short span of activity. And Jesus and Mohammed and others of that particular nature. I speak of them in terms of wisdom, not in terms of . . .

SL: Yes, because some people would regard that as a blasphemy . . .

HJ: Yes, I speak of them in terms of the wisdom that they brought to the civilization. They affected vast civilizations in very short amounts of time without the vast capabilities that we currently have in this civilization.

SL: How do you react to the suggestion, though, that it tends to be, looking around there, an awful lot of Scientologists are post-war people and youngsters . . .

HJ: I'm not.

SJ: No, well, that's a backhanded kind of compliment then . . .

HJ: No, I just had to throw that in . . .

SL: . . . and you're not getting the stats up, as they would say, and that in fact there's been a slight sign of a deflation in membership. Perhaps the actual management of resources has been dumped, very effectively financially, to keep the ship afloat. But unless the new people are coming in, it's going to be like a large company that's not having a cash-flow.

HJ: I've heard that and let me tell you I've just been through Milan and off over into Rome and Paris, Denmark, Munich, Germany and so forth. There are currently internationally — I don't know about other religions: have no measuring stick here so I'm caught without a . . . but I know that we get 12 to 13,000 new people walk through our churches every week, every week. Out of those we have some 8,000 take a course of some kind, miniature not major, but a course of some kind every week. . . . It doesn't mean that each person there becomes a hard and fast Scientologist but he gains a certain piece of wisdom, knowledge, applicability for life that he's never had before and he uses it. You have to look at it that way. He's changed back to the two-idea concept that can be implemented by better communication, which is our final goal. What is the assimilated rate of change in a civilization given the exponential expansion of that capability in the society? Just that one factor. Now this is a mathematical view computation. The CIA (God love their dirty black hearts because I don't) did a secret computer analysis at Stamford Research Institute probably 7 or 8 years ago in which they set up a computer model to analyse the effects of religions and newer religions on civilization and carried it out for 750 years.

So . . . when you ask me the question of our survival I have to somehow figure into that computation the opposite designs that the CIA might control — that's the negative factor. I don't know if this makes sense.

SL: . . . also there were people who were doing . . . shall we say, almost deprogramming type things to people who were stepping out of line within Scientology.

HJ: In what sense?

SL: Well, allegations about people who were sent . . . washing floors and eh . . . penances in the Catholic sense.

HJ: Well, I didn't find it terribly humiliating. In fact, it was kind of therapeutic. I happen to love working with wood, sanding doors . . .

SL: But it's difficult for outsiders to understand that. Isn't it like disciplining naughty schoolboys?

HJ: No, not at all. No, I think it goes back to the Buddhist concept . . . where a person contributes . . . to the group that he has in some way dishonoured or marked. You see what I mean?

SL: Yes.

HJ: But not in a . . . how shall I say it ? . . . not in a sense of eternal obsequiousness . . . or any of those things. It was a restorative step of capabilities; it's like one sorts out in a very sequential kind of way . . . understanding his own personal self, his involvement if you will . . . . To sin originally in its concept meant 'to miss the mark'. Well, when you're going towards the wrong mark it's a corrective kind of thing . . . I think the first time I did it I was terrified to have to go . . . first of all that I had been . . . I felt that I had fallen that far down as me. But then I saw the sense of it, then I saw that it was not abusive at all; it was not abusive and there is something to be said about good old physical labour. Washing the walls or mopping a floor or working with woodwork or laying bricks or . . . you know, these are the things that I remember as a kid, I absolutely enjoyed tremendously.

SL: But from the point of view of someone who has, if you like, left the organization; they look back and they see it as a kind of tyranny, don't they?

HJ: Some do. . . .

And so the conversation went on. Heber Jentzsch loved talking —

and he talked well. A born preacher, he is now the equivalent of honorary prophet cum Public Relations executive rolled into one. The man's warmth and humour are obvious. When I threw him an awkward question he would digress into a long discourse, usually on the rights of religious freedom and the mentality of those who were attacking the Church of Scientology. The actor in him relishes the drama of the clash between Scientology and its opponents. The preacher in him vituperates against the men of sin who dare to oppress his religion. As we drove on to Gilman Springs, Heber talked in dark apocalyptic terms about genocide, 'Gestapo' and Nazis. The irony was that these are the very analogies used against Scientology by its enemies. He was using them to describe his idea of the shadow which confronted the Church of Scientology.

A tarantula scuttled across the surface of Highway 79 as we drew near to Gilman. The land was flat and dry, stretching towards small hills in the west. 'We had to put security in at Gilman,' Heber explained, 'because some guy was firebombing the area with a book of matches.' The opponents of Scientology have described the security at the Gilman complex as rather like a prison camp. I soon saw that they had vastly overstated their case. Certainly there were seven foot high wire fences round the perimeter and the gates were manned by two security guards in brown uniforms, checking passes. It was odd for a church, but not for a film studio. A film studio is exactly what Gilman Springs had started as, making films at Hubbard's direction under the title of Golden Era Studios.

I was taken on a tour which wound up in the recording studio which has been equipped with a synthesizer. At the keyboard, conjuring a wizardry of sounds and rhythms from the machine, was Barry Stein, an architect in his thirties who had been a member of the 'Apollo All-Stars' pop-group back in the shipboard days. Now his talents were in making tapes but he kept his hand in as an architect. The castle complex at Saint Hill was his work, as was the restored ballroom at the Fort Harrison Hotel in Clearwater. Occasionally Heber Jentzsch would stop and talk to one of the Gilman staff. We sipped orange juice and I admired the facilities, the replica clipper-ship, the view and everything else in sight. It was all so tranquil. Like a leisure complex. But somewhere here lived David Miscavige, the man they said did not have any power but who could depose the founder's wife and order Hubbard's son Arthur[1] and his wife to be his personal servants. It was

[1] One of Hubbard's four children by his third wife, Mary Sue.

difficult to reconcile that picture with the Gilman that I saw.

My stay in Los Angeles was extremely pleasant and that night I dined with Heber Jentzsch and his second wife Karen, also a leading Scientologist. We were the guests of Marshall Goldblatt, an English property dealer who had taken many of the Scientology auditing courses. They had changed his life, he smiled, and the benefits which he obviously was prepared to rain down upon the Church of Scientology were but scant reward. It was all so agreeable.

The only jarring note was when I called in on my last day to pick up some photocopied material from a shop suggested to me by Michael Flynn. It was run by 'squirrels' and when my escort reported this back to her seniors, I was shown into a large room in the Cedars complex and seated round a large table with several Scientologists, including Heber Jentzsch. Into the room came a lean young man wearing a white short-sleeved shirt, the Sea Org kit. His eyes were wild and staring. Who was I? What was my connection with this squirrel group? What kind of book was I going to write? The eyes grew wilder. The pressure was stepped up. The atmosphere became electric. I was being interrogated. Across the room from me on the opposite wall was a photograph of Hubbard and underneath a quotation from a policy directive of February 1966 — 'Don't ever submit tamely to an investigation of us. Make it rough on attackers all the way.' The young inquisitor's name was Ken Hoden and he was then in charge of the Office of Special Affairs in Los Angeles. My contact with the 'squirrels' had revealed me as a potential enemy.

I managed to appease my interrogator by offering to leave the materials I had purchased so that the org could supply me with a list of any errors which the Scientologists felt were contained within them. This seemed to satisfy Mr Hoden and the files disappeared. Since then (September 1984) they have not been returned to me despite repeated requests. Various reasons were given but eventually I was told apologetically by a friendly official that it was not church policy to help those who dealt with 'squirrels' and this was why the Los Angeles org had retained the files.

Having survived my interrogation, I flew back the next day to Boston where I was to meet the two men the Church of Scientology regards as its deadliest enemies — attorney Michael Flynn and psychiatrist Dr John Clark.

6 Mindbenders and Faithbreakers: Scientology and Psychiatry

'THE DAY Thou gavest, Lord, has ended. The darkness falls at Thy Behest.' The three hymn singers gathered round the small organ in the spacious split-level lounge of the New England house on a Sunday evening were singing lustily. Through the open windows the voices drifted down to a small lake surrounded by trees where their daughter had played as a child. Now in her thirties, she was seated at a harpsichord, while her father played the organ and her mother led the singing in which I joined. It was September 1984. The music-loving family lived in the fashionable village of Weston, Mass., a few miles southwest of Boston. Their name — Clark. Six months earlier, the father of this family was described on Radio Station WXKS by Heber Jentzsch in the following terms: 'He was talking in a court process and basically he was asked, "Well, how do you feel about the worship of Satan?" and basically he indicated that was therapeutic. And then they said, "What about the worship of God?" and he indicated that was destructive.' The quiet-voiced man with the greying beard who was playing hymns at the organ and singing was Dr John G. Clark Jr., M.D., private psychiatric practitioner and Assistant Clinical Professor of Psychiatry at the Harvard Medical School, Boston. It was hard to reconcile the softly spoken sixty-year-old man I met with the picture I had been given by the Scientologists. Indeed, I was carrying a briefing file on Dr Clark's 'crimes' which the Church of Scientology had supplied. They ranged from writing for the American *Atheist* magazine, to being involved in 'deprogramming' (the controversial technique to break an individual's involvement in religious cults). Further crimes were giving diagnoses without having met the patient and of 'genocide' in his attempt to destroy a religion. On investigating these charges, I found that none was well founded.

Certainly Dr Clark has been active in many of the key lawsuits against the Church of Scientology and even gave expert psychiatric evidence at the Justice Latey hearing in England in 1984 which resulted in the judge attacking Scientology publicly. Dr Clark is also one of the moving spirits behind the American Family Foundation, an anti-cult organization which is based in nearby Riverside, Mass., and which exists as a charity to disseminate information on cults and assist families with members involved in them. Despite his modest manner he is a determined and stubborn opponent of Scientology on whom the Church of Scientology has played many dirty tricks, including raking through the dustbins at his home, where he also has his consulting rooms, in an attempt to gain confidential material. In 1985 he counter-attacked by suing the Church of Scientology for $35 million for attempts to destroy him both professionally and personally. If the John G. Clark file which I was handed was authentic, there is no doubt that Dr Clark should not continue to command respect as a witness against Scientology, so before we hear his testimony, let us look at its contents.

First, the article in the American *Atheist* of May 1977. It was not submitted by Dr Clark. It *was* written by him and analyses the destructive influence of cults upon mental health, but was sent to the *Atheist* magazine by Scientologists, who then proceeded to use the connection as criticism of Dr Clark.

Second, is the charge of being involved with deprogramming. When I was in Los Angeles, I had been shown a video taken by Ted Patrick (alias 'Black Lightning') which had been subpoenaed in a court action against Patrick. It showed him forcibly restraining two young cultists, one a Scientologist, who had attempted to leave the room in which they were being 'deprogrammed' (a euphemism for roughly interrogated and brain-washed). It was not a pretty sight and Patrick has served jail sentences for his zealous efforts on behalf of parents which have included kidnap and assault. Whatever the shortcomings of many of the new religious movements, such as the Unification Church (the Moonies), Hare Krishna or Scientology, the use of such methods cannot be justified in any way whatsoever. However, the American Family Foundation do not practise 'deprogramming', as Dr Clark and the director, Dr Michael Langone, both told me. The photograph of Dr Clark sitting beside Ted Patrick at an informal Senate hearing in 1979 sponsored by Senator Robert Dole (which Scientologists show as proof of a liaison) was possible because Dr Clark was allocated that seat. He had no other dealings with Patrick.

The Satanism charge against Clark is based on remarks he made during cross-examination in the District Court Concord, New Hampshire, on 23 July 1980, during a lawsuit brought by Donald Kieffer against his former cult, the Moonies. It was the Scientologists themselves who supplied me wth the transcript, but as in so many other cases of documentary 'evidence' they produce, it does not always bear the interpretation they put on it.

Cross-examining Dr Clark, the Moonies' attorney, Jean-Claude Sakellarios, asked him if he believed that there is a devil. Dr Clark's testimony runs:

> **Dr Clark:** To people who are responding to that image in a vivid sort of way, the devil is a reality . . . the problem here is that I'm trying to deal with what people do, what their behaviour is, and to a degree relate whatever of their thought processes that may be expressed, to relate them to their behaviour. And if they wish to have a belief about the devil but they still don't sacrifice chickens to the devil, then anybody can believe in the devil.
>
> **Counsel:** That's healthy?
>
> **Dr Clark:** For some people it is perfectly healthy. There are all kinds of beliefs. I am not interested in people's beliefs unless they are made into acts that are egregious . . .
>
> **Counsel:** Do you think that believing in God is helpful?
>
> **Dr Clark:** I'm certain that it is helpful, but it's also been very very damaging for some people. It's how it is used. People then take the belief in God and take it all the way to him in human sacrifice. I would consider that, from my point of view, was bad behaviour. And its relationship to belief is interesting, but it's the behaviour that in court and open society is important.

The actual answer by Dr Clark does not bear the interpretation put on it by Heber Jentzsch. I was therefore somewhat wary of three affidavits by an attorney who had been involved in a lawsuit in which Clark testified, a law student who had heard his testimony and a Scientologist mother of a youth whose father was seeking to prise him from the Church of Scientology. Few direct quotes are made in these affidavits from court transcripts, but Dr Clark is accused variously of being unfamiliar with the practice and doctrines of cults about which he testifies, yet of saying they would mutilate minds.

Dr Clark's response to these accusations is that he has examined hundreds of cultists and has often been asked hypothetical questions, such as whether it is possible to be harmed over a long period of time, but that he has always been careful to give evidence within the bounds of an opinion.

Far more damaging is the other charge made by the Scientologists — that Clark is willing to give diagnoses without seeing patients and that he uses the very fact of cult membership as evidence of mental illness. In support of this, the Church of Scientology has circulated to every country where Dr Clark's opinions are quoted, a letter from the Complaints Committee of the Massachusetts Medical Board replying to allegations that Dr Clark had diagnosed a Hare Krishna devotee, Edward Shapiro, simply on the basis of his membership of the cult. The letter, signed by the chairman, George J. Annas J.D., states: 'the basis upon which this "diagnosis" was made seems inadequate, as mere membership of a religious organization can never, standing alone, be a sufficient basis for a diagnosis of mental illness'. Dr Clark points out that the Board investigated the complaint and decided to take no further action.

Other activities of the Church of Scientology against Clark were to try to cause trouble for him at the Massachusetts General Hospital where he enjoys consultant status, by implying to the Board that he was using the hospital's name in connection with his anti-cult activities and research. Dr Clark laughs this one off, pointing out that he enjoys the confidence of the administration of the MGH.

In Germany, the Scientologists tried to bring an action against Clark under the International Convention for the Prevention of Genocide because he was spreading theories that more than half the members of new religions were mentally ill, and was acting in a similar way to Nazi psychiatrists when they were engaged in annihilating religious minorities. The strong statements contained in their Press release linking Clark to the worst excesses of deprogramming were but one shot in a continuing campaign. Dr Clark alleges that he has received phone threats, false complaints filed about him as a physician and scurrilous rumours about affairs with female patients. There had been private investigators assigned to him, personnel records from a health centre where he worked were stolen and leaflets were handed out at MGH stating falsely that Clark believed in electro-shock therapy and that he had connections with the Nazi party. A reward of $25,000 was offered for information which would lead to a criminal conviction of Dr Clark.

The last straw for Clark came in 1985 when the Church of Scientology placed an advert in the *Boston Herald* of Tuesday, 19 February, headed 'Have your rights been violated by Dr John G. Clark?' It went on to suggest anti-religious activities and professional malpractice and asked respondents to contact the local Church of Scientology at 448 Beacon Street, Boston. Dr John Clark had had enough. He began a massive lawsuit for $35 million in damages against Hubbard, alleging defamation, invasion of privacy, malicious prosecution and finally conspiracy 'to silence plaintiff; to inflict severe professional, personal and emotional injury on plaintiff and if possible to destroy him completely.'

On hearing of the suit, the swashbuckling Heber Jentzsch responded in characteristic style. 'Dr Clark,' he said, 'is obviously suffering from paranoid schizophrenia and should avail himself of immediate electro-shock treatment so that [he] may demonstrate to the world the efficacy of such.' He repeated the charges that Dr Clark was engaged in a conspiracy against religion and hinted that he was involved with the CIA in this process. Since he had not visited a Church of Scientology, said Jentzsch, his scientific enquiry must be based upon clairvoyance.

Although Clark has not done research within the Church of Scientology, his involvement dates from the mid-seventies when he was called to testify in several cases involving cult members. He now feels he has seen enough of the casualties of the movement to be able to state categorically that Scientology harms the mind. Apart from that clinical stance, he goes further, charging a true lack of any tested scientific viewpoint for Hubbard's theories. But his moral indignation is aroused because 'from beginning to end they do not take responsibility for damage to individuals or their families'. His criticism comes under two heads: BEHAVIOUR and INTENT. 'Their intent is to bring in money. They push an individual who is about to take a course, or in it, to the point where they can't do without them. And they get a lot of money. They believe that their ideas are the only true ones that anybody should pay any attention to. Thus they act in an antagonistic way toward any who don't share their beliefs and act as if these people do not have rights.' But Clark adds that it is not simply money that Scientology craves — it is *control*: 'The testimonies of those inside who say their life has been changed for the better are not scientific evidence. I have seen people who have taken several years after exposure to get back peace of mind. There are many things that we would regard as anti-family — easy marriages and easy divorces. They work sometimes eighteen to twenty hours a day and there is strict control. They are told to look as if they are enjoying it, so it's impossible just looking in to know what's going on inside these people. Talking is not the only thing that goes on in auditing. There's the atmosphere. The whole set-up. The magic of assertions. The *intention* of the auditing is to change the way that the mind works. It's quite different from psychiatric intention, which is to return to the best capacity of which the mind is capable. Over and over again in history people have found out how to influence others. In the twentieth century there are so many therapies that the religious and spiritual aspect which came about from pushing the mind came to be seen as religion rather than than psychotherapy. One of the problems that came from that is that the pressure used on people for spiritual and therapeutic purposes can harm some. The celebrities are treated in a different way — the Ethics people don't come down on them. Their experience is that everything is OK. It's well known that the celebrities feed very well indeed. But when those who have to slave get into trouble they are really punished and hurt in so many ways, all the way to being locked up in chains. There's an underlying cruelty in the whole thing.'

I put it to Dr Clark that some of the 'slaves' I had seen seemed very happy, but he was undaunted. 'Even in the pre-Civil War days, slaves had their tasks, their place in the culture and they were not miserable by any means. It's the same with Scientology, which is a kind of slavery.' I suggested that apologists for the Sea Org would see it as a kind of monasticism and the authority of the Church of Scientology as akin to the control exerted by a hierarchical church over its monks and nuns. But Dr Clark was having none of that. 'The Roman Catholic Church at some of its worst times did play a lot of these sorts of games but today there is no such pressure. It's made harder to get in and there is a link with the family. I don't think the Roman Catholic Church is capable of hating families who have differences with the practice of the Church in the way that Scientology is.'

Dr Clark then made a theological point which placed Scientology acccurately within the religious spectrum. He called it gnostic — like many of the cults which existed around the time of Christ, peddling their brand of 'gnosis' or knowledge by which the follower could escape the handicap of this world. One of the catch-phrases of these groups was *'soma sema'* (a Greek pun meaning the body is a tomb). It resulted in disassociation of soul from the body, the latter being rejected as excess earthly baggage. Taken to its extreme, this theology meant that it did not matter what the body did by way of immoral acts: the 'soul' was 'saved' nonetheless. Dr Clark offered a partial explanation for the glaring discrepancies between Scientology theory and practice when he said, 'The gnostic does not care whether their mind survives.'

Dr Clark agrees that it is too easy to say that Scientology is not a religion at all but a con-game for making money and that its track-record disqualified it from being treated as a religion. It is more like a religion gone wrong — a monster which has been created out of the deep waters of the mind into which various pyschotherapies have been learned to fish with great success. Being 'born again' can now be achieved in a church or on a psychotherapist's couch. Dr Clark puts it thus: 'With the process of re-inventing these means of transforming comes a moment of inventing, a moment of genius. The inventor maybe says let me do this to help the family, health or some other. But because he has this power he must defend it and that leads to the "perfect and special power" over which I think that the cult leaders make their mistake — and I would have to apply that to Scientology and its leader.'

The irony about the battle between the psychiatrists and the Scientologists is that almost identical terms are used by each group about the other. The psychiatric lobby see the Church of Scientology as perverted religion. Scientology views them as persecutors of religion. The psychiatrists view auditing as a form of brain-washing, while the Church of Scientology says it is the American Family Foundation run by Dr Clark which is practising brain-washing by deprogramming members of new religious movements. Scientology proclaims that it is 'clearing the planet', a noble and humanist goal, while its critics see it as a destructive cult which breaks up families. Both groups cannot be right.

Certainly there is much that is on target about the criticism of psychiatry by the Church of Scientology. When Hubbard attacked 'brutal assaults on the brain' in the Dianetics era, he was undoubtedly ahead of his time. Nowadays the Church of Scientology gains public support for its campaigns on mental health issues such as ECT and the use of such drugs as Mandrax to treat psychoses. There were also the excesses of many freaky psychiatrists in the USA who regarded the possession of a couch as a licence to inflict all kinds of weird therapy including sex and nude romps. Hiding such perversion behind the cloak of medicine was rightly condemned. There was also legislation such as the Alaska Mental Health Act (introduced into the United

States Congress in 1955) which effectively removed the civil rights of any person who might be diagnosed as mentally ill and put psychiatrists into the position of secret policemen were this power to be abused. Scientologists call it the 'Siberia Bill' and claim Hubbard was instrumental in blocking it, incurring the enmity of psychiatrists. Subsequent champions of 'alternative psychiatry', such as Thomas Szasz (not a Scientologist), were able to argue that the growth of psychiatry was itself a source of much mental illness, the diseases emerging to fit the symptoms which had been invented by the psychiatrists.

Hubbard's case against the psychiatrists was summed up by him in an edition of *Freedom* magazine in 1970 (which now runs regular pieces by Szasz). He wrote: 'The psychiatrist, psychologist and their clerk, the sociologist, point out how bad things are getting and demand even more money. The patients who live get crazier and the State itself becomes imperilled and yet no psychiatrist or psychologist or their mental-health cliques ever pay back a penny of their unearned fees.'

Scientology saw itself as a radical alternative to psychiatry (Jentzsch's 'clash of two ideas') in which the Establishment was backing the enemy. Evidence that the CIA was toying with mind-control programmes in the fifties, later code-named MKULTRA, was uncovered by Hubbard who made the most of this as propaganda. This is presented as the reason government agencies have opposed Scientology. The excesses of the deprogrammers in kidnapping young cultists and subjecting them to interrogation sessions to 'break' their allegiance to their religion were further evidence of the Great Beast of psychiatry devouring their religion.

Another rebel psychiatrist who saw dangers from his own profession is Dr Lee Coleman who practises in Berkeley, CA. In a booklet, *Psychiatry the Faithbreaker*, he argues that the testimony of Dr Clark and other anti-cultists has encouraged opposition to new religious movements which amounts almost to persecution and denial of human rights. 'The anti-cult movement is asking Society to do the very thing it claims "cults" are doing. It asks Society to turn over independent-thinking to gurus. But in this case the gurus are psychiatrists. I see no difference between the outlandish claim that Jim Jones [the founder of a notorious cult whose followers committed mass suicide in Jonestown, Guyana in 1977] could cure cancer and the equally outlandish claim that a psychiatrist can tell an unwashed brain from a washed one. As long as we persist in elevating psychiatrists to the position of god-like wisdom we will be guilty of the same mistake made by those who turn over their independent thinking to someone else.' Dr Coleman compares the unquestioning way in which cultists swallow dogma from their guru to the way in which he was taught to accept everything Freud had said as gospel and concludes: 'Whatever events led up to the deaths of all those people in Jonestown, I am convinced that a major factor was this willingness of the congregation to turn over its decisions to one person.'

Although Dr Coleman's booklet is circulated and commended by Scientology, it is easy to that see that by this criterion of 'guru-centricity', Hubbard's minions stand convicted themselves. All the 'tech' was produced by Ron who wrote the policy, laid down how it should be run and, as we have seen, is still ubiquitous, if not omnipresent, in photographs and slogans on the walls of every org. His taped voice is played to inductees. Scientology is the conception, realization and organization of one man.

Most of the anti-cultists' activity is directed against the Unification Church, or Moonies. Most of the brain-washing literature draws extensively on Moonie methods with which we are not concerned here. It is also fair to add that generalizations about cult methods will not always do justice to the particular situation within a new religious movement. Even the anti-cultists acknowledge that alongside the destructive cults there are 'benign' ones. But despite differences of doctrine and style between the cults, there are common effects in the area which has come to be known as brain-washing and it is worth looking at some of these.

My guide was Dr Michael Langone, a psychologist who is Director of Research at the American Family Foundation in Weston, Mass. The AFF occupies a spacious basement of a wooden office block in the centre of this small village. Here the AFF produces its magazine *The Cult Observer*, which is a pastiche of cuttings of stories involving cults which had been published in newspapers. An extensive library and files on subscribers and supporters occupy other rooms. Dr Langone showed me into his tiny, windowless office and displayed the array of literature which the AFF has produced to help families, counsellors and those professionally involved with cults. The most concise of these booklets is *Destructive Cultism: Questions and Answers*, which is aimed mainly at parents of cult members. It states: 'Destructive cults can frighten a convert's family, deprive the convert of his autonomy and financial assets, interfere with his psychological development and impede the adjustment of those members who leave the group to return to mainline society.'

Dr Langone is not an advocate of 'deprogramming' because of the negative image which some practitioners have given it, but says he has seen too many young people who have benefited from it to condemn all forms of deprogramming. 'I prefer "re-evaluation counselling" to describe those converts who come out voluntarily and reserve deprogramming for the rescue/detention process. It might take many days of marathon sessions of talking to help someone reawaken their old personality, think critically and reconsider their cult involvement.' He conceded that one third of cultists leave voluntarily, another third after counselling and that the failure rate in deprogramming is high (one third), so the other methods are more likely to be effective anyway. Dr Langone rejects the charge that the AFF cannot tell an unwashed brain from a washed one. 'You can't deprogram someone who isn't programmed. The brain-washing is real but it's not all Korean War stuff. It's more complex than that and often takes place over years.'

It is here that the cult differs from a religious philosophy. The motives which make someone susceptible to a cult and the inducements which are offered to the convert are the desires and aspirations of the average person. The selling methods used are those of many products and organizations — and there is nothing wrong or remarkable in that. Some critics act as if the very act of wanting to interest someone in a new religion is suspicious in itself. If it were, totalitarianism would indeed have arrived, as the Scientologists claim. But the significant departure point is the factor of mind control. From the AFF studies it is possible to point to several ways in which the cult differs from simple religious philosophy.

In 'Religious Totalism: Gentle and Ungentle Persuasion under the First Amendment' (*Southern California Law Review*, November 1977) Richard Delgado argues that it is possible to draw a line between the cults and other acceptable forms of recruitment and proselytizing. 'The first is that religious cults expose their indoctrinees to a greater variety of classic mind-control techniques than other groups do, and apply these with greater intensity. Jesuit and other training institutions may isolate the seminarian from the rest of the world at various stages of the training period but the training does not involve physiological depletion nor does the order deceive the candidate concerning the duties required of members . . . the second answer concerns the end–state, or result, of religious mind control. . . . The legislative and judicial findings, first-person accounts by ex-cult members, case studies by psychiatrists and psychologists dispel any possibility of equating the effects of cult brain-washing with those of other groups and institutions. Television commercials may induce ennui and torpor but they rarely cause mental breakdowns; Jesuit training rarely results in broken bones, scabies or suicide.'

Delgado's study and those of the AFF psychiatrists and psychologists may seem too general to be precisely applied to any one cult. Equally the Scientologists could argue that these studies are perhaps applicable to the Moonies but not to them. They could, but they do not. Their position is that all the studies are misconceived and malicious persecution. Instead of arguing 'yes, that maybe is true but it doesn't apply to us', the Church of Scientology prefers to mount an all-out attack on the health professionals. It does not discuss the evidence but escalates the battle into an all-out war between the cults and their critics. The question then becomes one of the credibility of the psychiatric testimony, not whether it applies to Scientology. There follows a summary of the ways in which psychiatrists of the AFF describe the process of mind control practised by the cults in general. (I have added examples which may demonstrate their relevance to Scientology in particular.)

(1) Unending personalized attention by cult members in the initial phase *overload* the recruit's information processing capacity. This neutralizes his *critical thinking* during the courses, which attain a spurious sense of profundity and importance. The repetition of the drills time after time has a wearing down effect. Like soldiers being drilled the independent mind is depressed to the point where the recruit repeats what he is ordered to do unquestioningly.

(2) *Isolation* (residential courses or the ultimate isolation of shipboard life) gradually supplant the former life with the reality of life inside the cult.

(3) Traditional sources of *knowledge* are either *despised* or not present (the dictionaries to be found in every org course-room define words the Hubbard way. No reference material is permitted other than that written by Hubbard.) The org-speak is an alphabet soup of initials, jargon and pseudo-technical expressions. This heightens the impression that a science is being taught and that it is esoteric and unavailable to the bungling ignoramuses in the outside world.

(4) The long hours of courses and the *debilitating effect* of a beans and rice *diet and fatigue* cannot but play a part too in the weakening of independent thought. Constant pressure is kept up and breaks are strictly regulated.

(5) All this is reinforced by an authoritarian system and *punishment and reward*. The recruit's idea of how he is doing is not the criterion of success. Always there is the course supervisor whose approval must be sought. This regimentation teaches obedience from the beginning.

(6) The *esprit de corps* of the org is important also. *Group pressure*, especially the atmosphere of excitement that they are about to change the world, helps sweep the recruit onward. Joining the staff is regarded as proof of loyalty and seriousness of intent. Once the step of joining the staff is taken, the former world is rapidly left behind. Waking hours belong to the org, which furnishes friends, bosses and sources of information.

(7) Most powerful are perhaps *dissociative processes*. Auditing is the 'sacrament' of Scientology, the open sesame to advancement spiritually and within the hierarchy of the church. The non-staff member will have pressure put on him to take more and more courses, if necessary borrowing money to do so. The staff member can have more auditing without paying, but each hour on the E-Meter cans sharpens the sword of Damocles hovering above him should he leave and have to pay a freeloader bill. Auditing itself completes the process. The traumatic episodes in the recruit's past are teased out and put in front of him. The quick-fire questioning of the auditor forces the recruit through the process on the basis that Hubbard has outlined, i.e., if in the hothouse atmosphere of auditing he is told that a particular incident is from a past life, then that is the basis on which he deals with it — implicitly accepting the Scientology system.

The AFF sum up the manipulative factors used by cults under these heads: DENIGRATION OF CRITICAL THINKING; GROUP PRESSURE; DISSOCIATION; GUILT INDUCTION; REWARDS AND PUNISHMENTS. Taken together and promoted all day long, they constitute a powerful control process.

Another factor in cult techniques was identified by Conway and Siegelmann in *Snapping: America's Sudden Epidemic of Personality Change*, published in 1978. Crudely, their theory was that the conversion methods of the cults led to a point where the information overload, the peer pressure, the isolation, guilt, inadequacy, and all the rest, became impossible to resist. 'Snapping' took place and thereafter the recruit was deeply involved. It was as if the recruit's mind opened at this moment like a clenched oyster revealing the soft and vulnerable inner self into which the cult thrust its sour pearl of wisdom. Evangelical crusades employ the same technique but once 'Christ' is received the evangelist does not invoke an organizational control system to ensure adherence to him, which makes the difference between this and a cult. The technique was adapted by pop singer P. J. Proby from a southern Baptist preacher he had watched and he was able to 'work an audience' to the brink of hysteria. 'Snapping' within the cults is a more private, low-key affair. Conway and Siegelmann were among those who suffered lawsuits from the Church of Scientology for the application of their theory to Scientology.

The ordinary course-rooms I visited in Britain and America were not buzzing with any such hysterical enthusiasm, but Religious Studies researcher Sarah Hogge during her sojourn at Saint Hill recorded several such sessions. At the beginning of every day's study a passage by Hubbard is read aloud. Here is the transcript of a session in which the supervisor was 'Charles'.

> C: So take a seat . . . good. I have got a bit of LRH to read to you. It's from one of the Study Tapes, number 5, called "Evaluation of Information". OK? . . . "Now of course some of the teachers I had on the subject of anti-submarine warfare were busy teaching me how to build. How to build, if you please. There was a war going on. I didn't have any time to build anything. I tried to explain it to them . . . that's one of the things they taught me, and boy was I able to catch up on my sleep *[laughter]* because I just knew . . . that out there in the middle of the Pacific Ocean with my hands full of Jap submarines I was not gonna have to build one of these things. I was merely gonna have to know how to use it and, if necessary, repair it . . . I figured out that in the middle of action . . . that's all I would need to know about that equipment, so I had myself a nice sleep." *[laughter]*
>
> C: OK *[laughter]*, that's to give you an idea what you're gonna use the data for, rather than get stuck in an encyclopaedia for hours looking up something like physics which is not what we teach you here. OK?

Note the smiling endorsement of Ron's exploits as a war hero which, of course, are false.

After 'Scripture', the supervisor always asks if the class is ready to start. The following exercise is then performed, running through the 'tone-scale', which gets everyone laughing and generally hyped up. In this transcript the supervisor was still Charles:

> C: So are you ready to start? *[very brightly but only a few*

reply] Good. OK. So I want you to answer me in apathy.
OK? Are you ready to start?

All: Yeah *[general groans]*.

C: Good, Now answer me in grief. OK. Are you ready to start?

All: *[crying and wailing noises]*

C: Good. Now answer me in despair. Are you ready to start?

All: *[sighs]*

C: Good. Now answer me in fear. Are you ready to start?

All: *[wails of terror]*

C: Good. Now answer me in covert hostility. Are you ready to start?

All: Yeah *[in suspicious, so what's-it-to-you voices]*

C: Good. Now answer me in hate. Are you ready to start?

All: Yes *[shouts of anger]*

C: Good. Now answer me in pain. Are you ready to start?

All: Yes *[with gritted teeth]*

C: Good. Now answer me in boredom. Are you ready to start?

All: Yeah *[apathetic]*

C: Good. Now answer me in mild interest. Are you ready to start?

All: Yeah *[intonation rising]*

C: Good. Now answer me in strong interest *[the supervisor's voice becomes very enthusiastic]*. Are you ready to start?

All: Yes.

C: Now answer me in cheerfulness. Are you ready to start?

All: Yes *[enthusiastic]*

C: Good. Now answer me with enthusiasm. Are you ready to start?

All: YES *[shouted]*

C: Good. Now answer me in exhilaration. Are you ready to start?

All: YES *[shouted ecstatically]*

C: Good. Start.

Note the constant repetition of commands which is a feature of auditing, as we saw earlier, and all the other drills which must be carried out to the letter as Hubbard wrote them, right down to the responses of 'OK'. It is a strange study system which needs to work the students into a frenzy before they can put their intellectual powers to work, but, on the other hand, if the process is seen as manipulation of the emotions then it is perfectly clear what is going on. At the end of the afternoon there is another muster, at which students are encouraged to share their 'wins' with the others. In the following extract, the supervisor was called Pauline.

> P: Who's on target? *[All hands go up.]* Who's likely to make their target by the end of the day? *[All hands go up.]* Who'd have made their target if they hadn't been doing something else like drilling? *[All hands go up.]* OK, that's good. *[Everyone claps.]* Who'd like to share a win? *[All hands go up.]* Who's going to start the ball rolling?
>
> **German Girl:** I got the vision today that we're really gonna make it and that we're really gonna clear this planet and when we've done that we're gonna go on to other planets. It doesn't matter if people go on outside dropping the atom bomb. We're in here and we're up there and we'll carry on with this study. We'll really do something to save this planet that really feels good. *[Mass applause.]*
>
> **French Lady:** I'm right at the end of my Dianetics book and it gives me a much clearer insight into the auditing I got before and so it's very very good to see how it all worked . . . I've been happy right from the start of the training. *[Everyone claps.]*
>
> **American Lady:** I really enjoyed doing TRs today. I find it so much easier to look up these words. It's great. *[Laughter.]* I had some great wins today. *[Mass applause.]*

The whole atmosphere is one of mild hysteria. Zeal is rewarded. Staff are encouraged to inform on any ethics breaches by other Scientologists. Staff Scientologists received rewards of $400 to $1,000 for information leading to the return of the 'scriptures' stolen by Robin Scott.

Time and time again one comes across amazing contradictions within Scientology. There are those who want to 'clear the planet' and establish their new kingdom of heaven. There are the paramilitary uniforms and the interrogations by Ethics and Finance Police. There are the ordinary troops, some of whom are totally unaware of the terror-tactics employed by the shock troops. There are the symbolic echoes of occultism in the symbols and the interests of the founder. And there is the founder himself — paranoid and schizophrenic, yet a leader who could mesmerize and charm followers into fanatical devotion. The same question might be asked of Hubbard that many have asked about Hitler — was he mad or bad?

Attorney Michael Flynn is fond of using the Hitler analogy to

ove: The Church of Scientology complex at 3 Fountain Avenue, Los Angeles, formerly Mount Sinai Cedars of Lebanon Hospital

Below: Mrs Shirley Young *(left)* and Mrs Susan Jones, my guides in Los Angeles

Above: Dr John G. Clark, psychiatrist and
Assistant Clinical Professor at Harvard
Medical School

Right: Michael Flynn, the Boston attorney w
has been involved in numerous cases of
litigation against the Church of Scientology

Left: David Mayo, former senior aide to Hubbard, and now heading the breakaway movement of the Church of New Civilization in Santa Barbara

Below: Heber Jentzsch, President of the Church of Scientology International

Above: Church of Scientology Finance Police unloading surveillance equipment

Left: A security guard patrolling outside the Los Angeles HQ of the Church of Scientology

Above: Golden Era Studios at Gilman Springs, situated across the Highway

Below: Heber Jentzsch and the make up supervisor at the Golden Era Studios

Above right: Aerial view of the mock-up clipper-ship built at Gilman Springs, Southe California

Below right: The swimming-pool and clippe ship at Gilman Springs

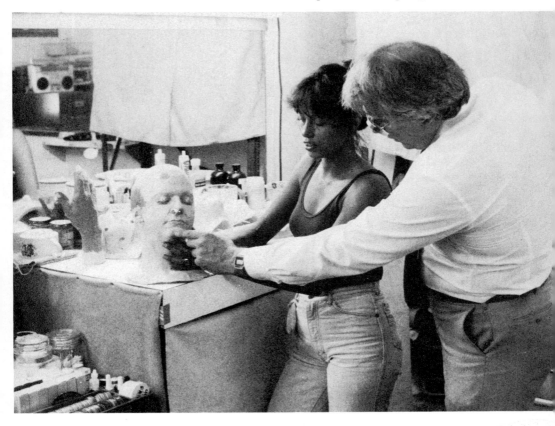

Above: The author photographed aboard the clipper-ship at Gilman Springs

Below: Most official photographs of Hubba published by the Church of Scientology sho him in the golden days of the *Apollo* voyag or earlier. This one, taken from a television documentary, in 1973, shows the 'Commodore' to be deteriorating rapidly

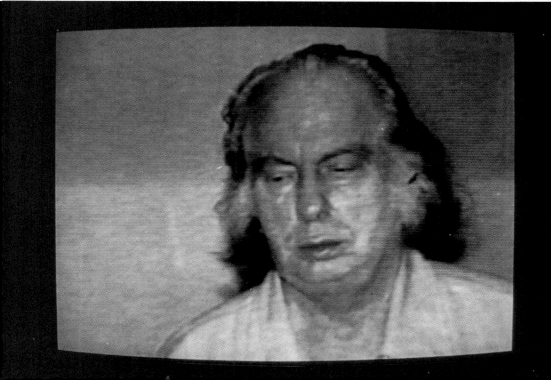

describe Hubbard. He cites the 'Suppressive Person' doctrine as a common device of dictators throughout history to eliminate their opponents. Flynn asserts that Hubbard's intentions were malevolent from the start and money and power were his objectives. As quoted earlier, Flynn says: 'The whole thing begins and ends in the mind and intentions of Ron Hubbard.' But was that mind diseased when it conceived the vision of Scientology?

Hubbard's estranged son by his first wife Margaret, Ronald DeWolf (alias 'Nibs' Hubbard), believes that it was. He has several times alleged that Hubbard, the great anti-narcotic campaigner, was himself a frequent drug user and even fed DeWolf phenobarbital in his bubble-gum to make him into a 'moon-child', prompted by his occult interests. DeWolf says his mother told him about his father's interest in the 1930s in PDH — which stands for Pain, Drugs, Hypnosis. Ron's use of it coupled with black magic was an effective form of brain-washing which he incorporated into his early Scientology materials. 'You'll see PDH throughout early Scientology literature,' DeWolf told Dennis Wheeler of the Santa Rosa *News-Herald* in 1982, describing the early days of Scientology as satyricon on tour, an orgy of black magic, drugs and the abuse of women followers. DeWolf, now in his early fifties, was a participant in this as Executive Secretary of the Church of Scientology. He has inherited his father's red hair and jokingly refers to himself in those days as 'the great red godlet'. His wife persuaded him to quit the church in 1959 and he has been estranged from his father since that time. To avoid Church of Scientology 'harassment' he changed his name in 1972.

In June 1983 he gave an interview to *Penthouse* magazine in which he detailed further charges of sado-masochism, black magic and fraud against his father. The credibility of DeWolf's testimony was undermined by a videotape made in November 1972 of an interview with Scientology official Arthur J. Maren in which DeWolf confessed that all the damning statements he had made previously about his father [in the sixties] were completely untrue. Asked several times whether he had been asked or forced to make this retraction, DeWolf asserted each time that he had contacted the Church of Scientology himself 'out of the blue' to make the recantation. When *Penthouse* published their article in June 1983, the Church of Scientology was in a strong position to demand a right of reply and in January 1984 the magazine duly ran an extended article by Heber Jentzsch puffing the merits of Hubbard. It would therefore be unwise to base any final assessment of Hubbard's mental state during the formative years of Scientology upon DeWolf's evidence.

There is, however, another testimony from one of those close to Hubbard: the divorce petition filed by his second wife, Sara Northrup, on 23 April 1951 in Los Angeles County Superior Court charges Hubbard with bigamy and torture. The original was inexplicably missing from the courthouse records but astute reporters from the *St Petersburg Times* tracked down a copy. In it she alleged that Hubbard presented himself as a bachelor when they married on 10 August 1946 in Chestertown Maryland, but that he was not divorced from his first wife, Margaret Grubb Hubbard, of Bremertown, Washington, until a year later. She claimed that Hubbard had conducted drug experiments on her and had even counselled her to commit suicide as he feared a divorce would harm his reputation. Margaret Hubbard died an alcoholic in 1963 but Sara remarried and has slipped into obscurity. That is a pity since she could now confirm whether or not the recantation she 'signed' on 11 June 1951 is genuine. In it she states: 'I have not at any time believed otherwise than that L. Ron Hubbard was a fine and brilliant man . . . I have begun to realize that what I have done may have injured the science of Dianetics, which in my studied opinion may be the only hope of sanity in future generations.' The *St Petersburg Times* comments: 'The statement bears the subtle marks of L. Ron Hubbard's handiwork. The stilted language is similar to his writing style and the recantation includes a sentence with the word "enturbulating" which is not to be found in a dictionary but sometimes appears in Hubbard's writings.' If Mrs Hubbard II is alive, she probably regards discretion as the better part of valour since she would be regarded as 'Fair Game' with a vengeance.

Mrs Hubbard III (Mary Sue Whipp) did not fare much better. When she became a liability to LRH's personal security after the Guardians' indictment, she was forced into isolation from her husband. Love and loyalty did not seem to extend to Mary Sue from either Hubbard or his lieutenants who are said to have treated her contemptuously. In his will they got nearly all his money, not her.

Hubbard's psychotic behaviour from the earliest years of Scientology does not depend only upon the tormented members of his immediate family. Ironically some of the evidence for Hubbard's psychotic personality was supplied to me by the Church of Scientology in a large dossier compiled to rebut DeWolf's allegations in the *Penthouse* interview, and is in LRH's own writing. DeWolf had made some rather lurid claims about Hubbard teaching hypnosis to a British politician (revealed later as the late Tom Driberg, a notorious homosexual) so that he could seduce boys, and that they had both been in the pay of the Russians who had supplied the money to buy Saint Hill Manor. In rebuttal of this allegation, and to prove that Hubbard was a loyal American, the dossier contains letters which Hubbard wrote to the FBI in March 1951 tipping them off about alleged Communist infiltrators within the Dianetics movement. Some, like Richard Halpern of New York, were 'only very faintly suspected due to small objections to our having loyalty oaths'. (Hubbard had insisted that all the HDRF employees should take an oath of loyalty to the US Government, forswear Communism and that copies of their fingerprints should be sent to the FBI. It was a gesture whch would have gladdened Senator McCarthy's heart.) But one other suspect listed in the letters is worth noting. It is Hubbard's own wife: 'Sara Northrup (Hubbard) . . . Had been friendly with many Communists. Currently intimate with them but evidently under coercion. Drug addiction set in, Fall 1950. Nothing of this known to me until a few weeks ago. Separation papers being filed and divorce applied for.' For caddish acts that takes some beating.

The early 1950s often found Hubbard writing to the FBI about plots against him. One reads as follows: 'About 2 or 3 o'clock in the morning my apartment was entered. I was knocked out, had a needle thrust in my heart to give it a jet of air to produce a coronary thrombosis and was given an electric shock with a 110 volt current. All this is very blurred to me. I had no witnesses.' He talked of Communist inspired plots to infiltrate Scientology by slipping LSD to members. By 1955 the FBI were wearying of this deranged informant and one letter has the notation 'appears mental' scrawled across it.

In 1947 Hubbard applied for psychiatric treatment himself, a fact which may come as a surprise to those who see him as the scourge of psychiatry. In a letter dated 14 October 1947 to the Veterans' Administration from his Hollywood address, he wrote: 'Gentlemen, This is a request for treatment. After trying and failing for two years to regain my equilibrium in civil life, I am utterly unable to approach anything like my own competence. My last physician informed me that it might be very helpful if I were to be examined and perhaps treated psychiatrically or even by a psychoanalyst. Toward the end of my service I avoided out of pride any mental examinations, hoping that time would balance a mind which I had every reason to suppose was seriously affected.' Hubbard goes on to tell of depression and suicidal tendencies and concludes 'Would you please help me? Sincerely, Ron Hubbard.' The letter was one of the documents seized in the 1977 FBI raid and it is not known whether Hubbard received treatment.

Whether or not the letter is a sick attempt to con the Veterans' Administration into upping his disability pension is not clear. However, within a few years Hubbard had developed his intense hatred for psychiatry. The explanation for this change of attitude may lie in the power struggle. In the early years of Dianetics, Hubbard attempted to win over the medical profession with Dr Joe Winter's help, but Hubbard's style put them off and in 1951 the New Jersey Board of Medical Examiners had initiated an injunction against the Elizabeth Foundation of the Dianetics movement for conducting a school of medicine without a licence. Wallis[1] (pp. 73-4) concludes: 'It was almost certainly as a result of the publicity given to this action that creditors of the Foundation began to demand settlement, leading to the reorganization and centralization of the Foundation at Wichita. Possibly as a result of this response from the established therapeutic professions, Hubbard has since demonstrated a marked antagonism to medical practitioners, and to psychiatrists in particular.'

The vehemence and black propaganda which were the hallmarks of Hubbard's paranoia were directed particularly at mental health organizations, which were high on the Scientology list of 'enemies'. He was convinced that a mysterious organization referred to as the 'Tenyaka Memorial' was co-ordinating attacks on Scientology worldwide and that the UK-based World Federation for Mental Health (WFMH) and the National Association for Mental Health (NAMH) were behind it. A number of the FBI documents deal with the hunt for the Tenyaka Memorial organization. The 'central handler', according to Hubbard in a memo of 6 May 1971 marked 'Secret', was the secretary of the NAMH, Mary Appleby. 'It is she who writes and phones her contacts to start attacks on Scientology,' said Hubbard and went on to suggest that these attacks were the work of a Nazi network of drug companies, banks and psychiatrists, aimed at conquering the world. One Guardians' Office directive against the WFMH dated 27 March 1974 — sent from Saint Hill to the US — reads. 'Now the secretariat is in Jamaica and I would like a mission sent to finish off the files and make quite sure we have cleared them out. As it is closest to your area, could you please select

---

[1] *The Road to Total Freedom*

missionaries with a decent cover etc so we can finish them off. What I am after is any files on Scientology, Dianetics, LRH etc that the WFMH has.'

Yet another irony about Hubbard's antipathy to psychiatry is that many of the ideas upon which Scientology is based seem close to classic Freudianism, i.e. trauma experienced in childhood which gives rise to 'engrams'. Indeed, the debt was acknowledged by Hubbard himself in *Certainty* (a critique of psychoanalysis), p. 4, published in 1962. 'The discovery of the engram is entirely the property of Dianetics. Methods of its erasure are owned entirely by Dianetics but both of these were pointed to by early Freudian analysis and hypnotism.' Wallis records that Hubbard was a skilled practitioner of hypnosis, although in DMSMH he distinguishes between returning and reliving in Dianetics from regression and revivification in hypnosis. However, the process of auditing is arguably para-hypnosis and auditors are enjoined to add a 'canceller' at the end of a session that any suggestion given by them during the suggestion will be nullified. What is unique to Scientology is the blend of the Freudian with the occultist framework, the pseudo-scientific terminology, and the Eastern idea of reincarnation.

There is no doubt that Hubbard's mind was fertile. His lengthy list of published work in science fiction is a testimony to that. Between the years 1930–50 he is purported to have written fifteen million words under some twenty pen-names. They may not have been works of outstanding merit but they sold. Where his genius lay was his ability to see a gap in the rising tide of new religions and psychotherapies and to write a system which could be floated in that market. From the foregoing it must be evident that it was mad genius. What flowed from it later, demonstrated that this genius was bad as well as mad.

7 Cops and Robbers: Scientology and the Law

'I DON'T like bullies. Especially Fascist bullies.' Boston attorney Michael Flynn was referring to his arch-enemy, L. Ron Hubbard. He lay back in his leather armchair and swung his feet up on to the desk among the stacks of documents. One wall of the small room is stacked with books, in the corner a spiral staircase connects the floors of number 12 Union Wharf, Boston, where Flynn and his partners have their office. It is a low, long building constructed right on the side of the wharf and as we talked, yachts bobbed up and down beneath the window on the west side of Flynn's office. He is a talker. The self-assured and fluent tone, the machine-gun rattle of facts and ideas, betray the prize-winning law student who has become a prosperous lawyer and Scientology's greatest enemy.

As the sun streamed in through his window on that September afternoon, Flynn told me in his Boston Irish accent what had started him on his crusade against Hubbard and his church. 'This girl came to see me in 1979. They were doing awful things to her. Then they started doing awful things to me.' The girl was a former Scientologist and resident of Nevada named Lavenda van Schaick and the 'awful' things included attempts to get Flynn disbarred. Then there was the time when Flynn's private plane mysteriously acquired water in the fuel tanks and was forced to make an emergency landing. Flynn has no proof that the Scientologists were behind it. However, he has his suspicions. These are vehemently denied by the Church of Scientology's President, Heber Jentzsch: 'It's nonsense.' He told me that the Church of Scientology had conducted expensive investigations which showed that light aircraft of the type owned by Flynn were prone to condensation in the fuel tanks.

With the record in dealing with opponents of Scientology it was not surprising that Michael Flynn should believe that he was singled out for some attention. Several complaints against him were filed with the Massachusetts Bar Association and private investigators put onto the scent. For a while Scientologists rented a flat opposite his office at Union Wharf and observed the clients who came and went. It was at this time that certain documents were, says the Church of Scientology, 'retrieved' from Flynn's wastepaper dustbin. 'Horse manure,' says Flynn. 'They were stolen from this office.' The documents in question were shown to me in a 'Flynn File' kept by the Church of Scientology. They relate to the setting up in August 1980 of a company styled FAMCO (Flynn Associates Management Corporation), which the Church of Scientology alleges was a front to sell shares in the hope of raising money to finance litigation against the Church of Scientology. The aim, they say, was to break Scientology by lawsuits across the country and make a profit by so doing. Flynn points out that the documents concerned three different activities and were conflated by the Church of Scientology to make it look as if he was illegally raising money for litigation. All complaints against him to the Bar Association have been dismissed and he has countered by suing the Church of Scientology for making malicious complaints.

One undeniable fact is that Michael Flynn has sought to maximize his lawsuits against Scientology by extending the so-called 'class-action' to a series of individual lawsuits brought by disaffected Scientologists around the USA. The research, the witnesses, the previous pleadings undertaken by Flynn, were to be used as an anti-Scientology prosecution 'kit'. One document 'retrieved' puts it thus: 'It is projected that this activity will generate a chain-reaction in bringing former Scientologists out of the woodwork as well as generate massive publicity to assist in this endeavour. The purpose of this activity is to substitute individual actions for the class action which is currently pending in the Federal District Court of Boston and which inherently involves problems relating to jurisdiction, conflicts of laws, and damages.'

As viewed by the Church of Scientology this was 'genocide of a religion' and persecution of a religious organization through the courts in direct contradiction of the First Amendment to the US Constitution which guarantees separation of churches from State interference. From the Flynn side it was prudent marshalling of his resources and an attempt to ensure that the members of the Church of Scientology did not escape culpability by slipping from state to state through legal loopholes. He was determined that their frauds and crimes would catch up with them. 'They can believe what they want,' protests Flynn. 'I have no axe to grind with their beliefs, but when their conduct becomes illegal and harms people then something has to be done. They can believe in thetans if they want, but they shouldn't be practising deceit in the street.'

Michael Flynn, as already mentioned, sees many parallels between the Nazis and the Scientologists. 'The whole thing is a house of cards, built on deceit. Most of us, if we screw up, are responsible. But not Hubbard. He thinks he has the right to lie. He has said that he has power which gives him the prerogative to lie, cheat and steal because he understands it better than the wimps of the world. It's there in his own handwriting.' Flynn acknowledges that there are many well-intentioned people who join Scientology. 'They are not brain-washed — it's just that they are deceived and don't want to look. Sure, you can have an interesting discussion with Heber Jentzsch about religious freedom, but it's got nothing to do with what's been going on for the past thirty years. If we believe absurdities, we commit atrocities,' 'Flynn continued, his rhetoric conjuring up a picture of the enemy he has never met, L. Ron Hubbard. 'He *is* like Hitler, a fanatical leader demanding obedience. There's the parallel.'

I put it to him that there would always be those who believed the earth was flat or that they were reincarnations of Pharaoh. 'Sure, there are people who change their attitudes because of faith. But LRH will tell you that faith has nothing to do with Scientology. It's about processes, the tech correctly followed.' It is a telling theological point, made by a lawyer, for Scientology does indeed not depend on the level of belief or of moral goodness; it says that if you follow certain procedures you are assured of spiritual progress. Flynn further argues that the animosity of ex-Scientologists who are his clients is not the pique of disaffected believers who have rebelled from their allegiances. 'A person who believes in Christianity or Islam has faith through a doctrinal structure. It has nothing to do with whether Mohammed had a degree in nuclear physics, but if you're living with someone who says he has — and you should believe what he says because he knows — and then you find his statements are all nonsense, as Gerry Armstrong did, then that's not a disaffected believer. That's a guy who has discovered a fraud.'

Flynn has found the Armstrong case to be a goldmine of material to substantiate his charges against Scientology. 'There are thousands of documents which prove that the guy is a complete flim-flam.' Armstrong was his client and formerly a Hubbard aide assigned to shred a mountain of documents relating to Hubbard's personal file when there was a threat in the wake of the FBI raid that more documents might be seized in an attempt to incriminate Hubbard himself. However, on Armstrong's initiative, many were kept back to assist in the biography which writer Omar Garrison was commissioned to produce on LRH, with Armstrong as his researcher. When he began to discover that many of the documents did not verify claims being made by the Church of Scientology about Hubbard's achievements, Armstrong suggested to his superiors that this was undermining the reputation of LRH, which he still held at that time in high esteem. But his warnings went unheeded and Armstrong soon became disaffected. He left Scientology, taking many documents with him which he claimed would help to vindicate him and defend himself against attacks from the Church of Scientology.

The church, in the person of Mary Sue Hubbard, sued for the return of these documents, accusing Armstrong of theft and invasion of privacy. Judge Paul Breckenridge could not pass up the opportunity to comment on the irony of Mary Sue's complaining about invasion of privacy when she had, as Guardian supremo, been responsible for invading the privacy of others.

As the case proceeded it became clear that Armstrong had collected some very damaging materials. Despite protestations that the culling of pc folders for damaging information had been discontinued after the overthrow of the black sheep among the Guardians, testimony was heard that Lyman Spurlock was still culling pc folders well into 1982. The judge ruled that Armstrong had been justified in retaining the documents and awarded costs against the Church of Scientology. He also directed that many of the incriminating documents should be kept under seal pending further litigation when they might be required as evidence. These included items described as: '4-E Hubbard handwriting admissions re: control over mankind and naval background; 5-0 Hubbard re: forcing Mayor to resign March 22 1978; 4-K Hubbard handwriting black magic incantations; 6-L Handwritten re: open up a total war on IRS Gestapo tactics.'

In his summing-up dated 20 June 1984, Judge Breckenridge said: 'In addition to violating and abusing its own members' civil rights, the organization [Church of Scientology] over the years with its Fair Game doctrine has harassed and abused those persons not in the church whom it perceives as enemies. The organization clearly is schizophrenic and paranoid, and this bizarre combination seems to be a reflection of the founder, LRH. The evidence portrays a man who has been a pathological liar when it comes to his history, background and achievements. The writings and documents in evidence additionally reflect his egoism, greed, avarice, lust for power, and vindictiveness and aggressiveness against persons perceived by him to be disloyal or hostile.'

Flynn sees the case, against which the Scientologists appealed, as representing a milestone in the decline of Scientology. The Church of Scientology's response was to redouble its attacks on Armstrong's credibility. It accused him of being incomplete in his research on Hubbard's naval career and mounted a covert operation to expose him as a Government agent. The *Freedom* newspaper, a Scientology publication which specializes in attacks on the IRS and psychiatry, in May 1985 printed a splash 'exposé' of Armstrong as a Government intelligence operative who was involved not only with Flynn, but with the FBI and IRS in a plot against Scientology. They claimed this was a police sanctioned 'sting'. (The FBI had informed the authorities that they intended to gather evidence of criminal conspiracy against the Church of Scientology.) The exposé consisted of a secretly video-taped conversation in Griffith Park, Los Angeles on 7 November 1984 between Armstrong and a Scientologist, code-named 'Joey', who claimed to be asking his help in setting up a dissident group. The transcript of the conversation reveals Armstrong telling Joey the names and telephone numbers of several FBI and Justice Department officials handling various investigations involving Scientology. It is no surprise that Armstrong knew these. During the lengthy court proceedings in which he was involved, it is likely that all the opposition team would have been in touch with Armstrong for access to his material, to assist their own cases against the Church of Scientology. However, *Freedom* presents this as evidence that he was working for these agencies. Much more damaging is the charge that Armstrong encouraged 'Joey' to plant false evidence on Scientology files and that he was skilled in this technique himself. Here is what *Freedom* prints (Vol. 17, No. 10 May 1985, US Edition):

> **G.A.:** An organization's comm [communication] lines are of various kinds and I think you can use this fact — you know, realize what their comm lines are and plug into them . . . you see, because I think that during a part of this, we can simply create these, you know — I can create documents with relative ease. You know, I did it for a living!

JOEY: Great, so what kind of stuff are we going to create and who's going to get it?

G.A.: That's what we need to talk about . . .

This charge is extremely damaging to Armstrong as a credible witness if true. Yes, IF TRUE, because I obtained a loan of a copy of the video taken in Griffith Park from the Church of Scientology and it contains *no such passage*. The transcript on page 18 of *Freedom* begins at time-code 23:16 on the video clock, which would reveal if it had been edited or not. Armstrong goes on to say: 'We have not discussed anything about the destruction of the tech, right?', which occurs at 23.50. *Freedom* prints this as 'We have not discussed that Scientology is bad . . .' The video then continues at 24.12: 'It seems to me that you don't have a way of printing anything to get an issue on the lines, right? I'm saying I can do it! I can type those goddam things and duplicate them and make them look exactly the same!' All the intervening words in the *Freedom* transcript, some 400 words, do not occur at all on the video. Armstrong could be talking about fraud at 24.12 but he could be talking about sending a message, like the Dane Tops letter, which would appeal for support. Why did *Freedom* put in these passages, except perhaps to do a little false document insertion themselves?

One of the names mentioned to 'Joey' by Gerry Armstrong was an Assistant US Attorney named Brackett Denniston. According to *Freedom*, he was 'assigned' to investigate an attempt by Boston lawyer Michael Flynn to pass a two million dollar forged cheque on an account of Scientology founder L. Ron Hubbard. Denniston stone-walled the investigation into Flynn's involvement in the crime. 'To this day,' *Freedom* alleges, 'he has not followed up on the volumes of per-suasive evidence given to him by church attorneys and their investi-gators exposing Flynn as one of the perpetrators of the crime.'

The 'evidence' in question was supplied by one Ala Tamimi from the United Arab Emirates, a proven con-man who is serving a prison sentence in Italy while four other countries are queuing to bring charges against him. Tamimi must have seemed like a gift from the gods to the Church of Scientology when he came forward to say that he could describe how Michael Flynn had conspired with him to pass the bogus cheque, which was not accepted by the Middle East Bank in New York when Tamimi and his brother Akil tried to pass it in early 1982. Widely thought to be an attempt by Church of Scientology officials to 'loot' Hubbard's cupboard, this allegation was used by Flynn as evidence in a probate case brought by Ronald DeWolf that

Hubbard was not alive or unable to manage his affairs. But Ala, dubbed 'The Prince of Fraud' by the *Boston* magazine of 22 October 1984, took the Church of Scientology for a ride by asking for an advance payment before he gave them his 'evidence'. Then he fled with $25,000 of org money while Flynn was left to answer the charges, which were widely publicized on 23 July 1984.

Flynn's response was to slap a very large lawsuit on those who had been involved and for good measure he threw in another against the *Boston Globe* for $10 million for defamation damages when they ran the story supplied by the Scientologists despite being advised that the allegations were false. 'Prior to 23 July I'd never heard of Ala Tamimi,' says Flynn. 'It's a frame-up. He's a con. They (Church of Scientology) are a con.' Currently Flynn is personally involved in a lawsuit for $141 million against Hubbard. The Church of Scientology boasts that despite his ubiquitous battle against the cult, Flynn has never won a case against the church. But he has not lost one either, and the reason that such a claim can be made is that so many of the cases drag on for years and even when decided, there is an immediate appeal.

This raises the question of how a prosperous lawyer can afford to pursue a campaign against the Church of Scientology without financial reward. The Scientologists are quick to supply an answer. They point to a donation of $135,000 in 1983 from the New York Community Trust to the Scientology Victims' Defence Fund, which is administered from Flynn's office. At first sight it looks peculiar. The Scientologists claim the source of the recommendation was an aide of Nelson Rockefeller who had clashed with them back in 1955 over the 'Siberia Bill'. Heber Jentzsch raged, 'The Rockefellers backed Adolph Hitler during the Second World War and continue this tradition in present time by backing straw men who attack religious men and churches. Let it be known that we will vindicate Mr Hubbard's good name regardless of how many Rockefeller mega-bucks are poured into the Fund.' These turn out to be weasel words when the donation is measured alongside the hundreds of others of a humanitarian nature handed out by the Trust, totalling $350 million. There is already ample evidence in this book to show that many people have been harmed by Scientology and surely Michael Flynn, whatever his motives, cannot be expected to go on year after year charging nothing for his services. Until auditing is given away free the Scientologists have little to complain about. Their attempts to discredit Flynn have been shown up time and again to be sleazy and inaccurate at the very least.

Nor can they say that they have much more success in the court-rooms, as a review of outstanding cases reveals:

LAVENDA VAN SCHAICK, the girl whose case brought Michael Flynn into conflict with the Scientologists originally, brought a 'class action' on behalf of Scientology drop-outs alleging mind control, unlawful electronic surveillance and the leaking to the media of details of her private life obtained during auditing. The action was originally brought in December 1979 for $200 million but was settled out of court on 10 June 1985 for $150,000 just before it was due to go on trial before a jury in Boston. Church of Scientology President, Heber Jentzsch, said that the Judge, W. Arthur Garrity Jr., had forced the church to settle because he denied church motions to sequester the jury and to disqualify Van Schaick's lawyer, Michael Flynn, from the case. The bid to sequester was based upon reports of alleged phone-calls received by members of the jury which had awarded damages against the Church of Scientology in Portland, Oregon, earlier in the year (see below). The Church of Scientology attorney Harvey Silverglate filed a document with the court saying that Judge Garrity had libelled the church and its members and that they would not receive a fair trial in his court.

This was not the first time that Scientology had come into conflict with a judge assigned to one of its cases. In the mid-seventies the Guardians had hatched a plot to lure Federal judge Ben Krentzman, who was assigned to one of its Clearwater cases, onto a yacht stacked with prostitutes and film him in compromising situations. It did not happen, but a vicious campaign against the judges assigned to the trial of the eleven Guardians is outlined in an article in *The American Lawyer* of December 1980.

The first judge assigned to the case was DC District Court Judge George Hart Jr, who, back in 1976 in connection with one of the many Freedom of Information Act (FOIA) suits filed by the Church of Scientology, had casually proposed that a deposition be taken from Hubbard. This led Church of Scientology officials to think that the Government had something on LRH and were setting a trap. This sparked off not only 'Operation Snow White', already mentioned, but clandestine operations against all judges involved in FOIA suits and all DC District judges, designed to dig the dirt on their backgrounds and look for possible 'buttons' (org-speak for vulnerable areas) which might be used to obtain recusal motions which would force the judge to back down from the case if the Church of Scientology thought it was not going its way. Hart was the first victim of the recusal strategy. By telling him that he had been the target of such an illegal operation, Church of Scientology attorney Leonard Boudin effectively forced him to admit, 'I was afraid a jury would be prejudiced against the defendants because of their alleged threats against me.'

Hart stepped down and was replaced by Judge Louis Oberdorfer, who asked for any objections at the outset, whereupon the Church of Scientology reminded him he had worked for the tax division of the Justice Department in 1969 when it had ended the tax-exempt status of the Church of Scientology in Los Angeles. He stepped down on 5 February 1979 and was replaced by Judge Charles Richey. Intensive covert operations using private detectives with tape recorders swung into action and by the time the first nine defendants had been found guilty, the Scientologists were ready with their ammunition in the form of interviews which allegedly linked Richey in titillating detail with a prostitute at the motel at which he had stayed during the Los Angeles hearings. The story was leaked to the newspapers and five days later, on 23 July 1980, Judge Richey was admitted to hospital with exhaustion and pulmonary embolisms. Three down. In came Judge Aubrey Robinson. Richey's sentences against the 'DC 9' stood, but Robinson, too, was the target of a recusal motion on 5 September 1980. He survived to preside over the trial of the remaining two Guardians, Mo Budlong and Jane Kember.

There have been a variety of lawsuits brought by individuals against the Church of Scientology, among which are:

THE BATTLE OF WOUNDED KNEE: This was a lawsuit brought in October 1980 by Lawrence Stifler, a Boston marathon runner who had been obstructed as he was running by an over-zealous Scientology recruiter and had fallen, injuring his knee to the extent that he claimed he might never run again. His demand of $1.25 million damages was more modestly assessed by a jury in October 1984 as meriting $1,000 and medical expenses of $712.

TONJA BURDEN was twenty in April 1980 when she filed a $16 million suit alleging that she was used as slave labour by Hubbard in the CMO and was kidnapped after she escaped. This was the case which forced Hubbard to go into hiding from Gilman in 1980. The requested damages rose in 1985 to $45 million.

PAULETTE COOPER, as we saw in Chapter 4, was up there among the chief enemies of Scientology and was high in the damages stakes with a suit for $55 million when Flynn became her attorney. In 1982 she participated as one of his star witnesses in the Clearwater hearings (at which the Church of Scientology declined to testify since it could only put its case at the conclusion). Flynn, she now says, persuaded her that she should name Hubbard in her suit since he would not appear and therefore she would win by default or because the Church of Scientology would pay up rather than produce Hubbard. But in a dramatic reconciliation with its old enemy in 1985 the Church of Scientology proudly announced that it had settled all cases for and against Ms Cooper and brandished an affidavit in which she says Flynn misled her into thinking Hubbard was still in charge of the Church of Scientology and had used her in a strategic campaign. In the elaborate game of bluff and counter-bluff, accusation and recusal, perhaps nothing should surprise the observer of Scientology. It would be nice to think this was a story of reconciliation, a truly religious story with a happy ending, but judging by the tactics adopted by the Church of Scientology to discredit Ms Cooper, I am inclined to think it is more likely the case of a psychologically battered woman throwing her towel into the ring.

HOMER SCHOMER was formerly Treasury Secretary of ASI (Author Services Inc.) and his lawsuit names Hubbard, ASI, and includes David Miscavige and Pat Broeker who had subjected him to a ten-hour 'Sec-Check' and threatened him that he would go to jail when he showed reluctance in doing his job. This was to prepare fictitious invoices for services rendered to ASI by Hubbard. In the period during which Schomer did this (March–November 1982) Hubbard's personal assets grew from $10 million to $44 million. Schomer's own suit is for a cool $226 million.

It is difficult to feel sympathy for the 'victims' of Scientology who ask for this extravagant level of damages when many of them are young, healthy people who have all their mental faculties (brainwashing notwithstanding). When maimed victims of criminal violence obtain a pittance in comparison with disaffected Scientologists it is difficult to avoid the conclusion that greed is at the back of their minds. In other words, they have acquired a little of the avarice of the man they once admired and now despise, LRH himself. Certainly the American system is very different from anything we are used to in Britain. Damages sought are far in excess of those which are probable, on the aim-high-and-settle-for-lower principle. There is also the widespread practice of the lawyer getting a percentage 'cut' of the damages — in my view an extremely unjust practice, which possibly compromises the integrity of any lawyer operating on such a basis. One could argue that with these ludicrous sums the Church of Scientology is only getting a taste of its own medicine and that its extravagant claims are being taken at face-value. That valuation may mean paying through the nose. However, one case decided during 1985 excited the Scientologists to a fury of protest and even attracted sympathy from sources not normally associated with the Church of Scientology.

The case in question was brought first in 1977 in Portland, Oregon, by a young girl, JULIE CHRISTOFFERSON, who since that date has married and is known as Julie Christofferson Titchbourne. She was seventeen years old when she first took Scientology courses for nine months between 1975–6, during which time she completed a basic course and started, but did not finish, another one, and paid $3202 for books and materials. She left Scientology and was, with parental help, subsequently 'deprogrammed'. This led her to claim damages against the Church of Scientology because it had made fraudulent claims that it would improve her eyesight and raise her intelligence. The case seemed to set a precedent in that claims made by religious organizations could be considered subject to laws governing consumer goods.

At first the lawsuit asked for a modest $30,000 but this soon grew and Julie was awarded $2 million in damages in 1979. The Church of Scientology successfully appealed against the decision and a re-trial was ordered. Thus we reach a point in 1983 when Ms Christofferson, now claimant (Mrs) Titchbourne, made her eighth change in the damages sought. She asked for $43 million. The trial proceeded with attorney Garry McMurry representing her, and Earle Cooley for the Church of Scientology of California. Julie had added a request for damages against Hubbard himself to her suit.

The trial dragged on with sometimes weeks elapsing without Julie being mentioned in proceedings, the testimony being of a general nature relating to Hubbard, the RPF, the culling of pc folders and other examples of Church of Scientology misconduct. It soon became clear that it was the Church of Scientology itself which was on trial. That made the case of more than passing interest.

On Friday, 17 May 1985 the jury announced its verdict — $39 million damages, of which $20 million were awarded against Hubbard personally. All hell broke loose. The Scientologists howled that this was an attempt to wipe out a religion, while McMurry rejoiced, 'The award will stand and be heard around the world.' He called the amount 'adequate for the harm that was intended'. Immediately thousands of Scientologists from all over America assembled in Oregon for peaceful protests against the decision which, before becoming final, still required the ruling of Judge Donald Londer on a motion by the Church of Scientology for a mistrial. Celebrities such as John Travolta flew into Oregon in his Lear jet to join in the carnival of dissent. Jazz pianist Chick Corea cancelled a concert to protest on behalf of his religion.

The question of whether Scientology was a religion was central to the arguments for a mistrial. Judge Londer ruled at the outset that it *was* a religion but told the jury that they could find that while some statements made by Scientology were religious, others were secular and therefore subject to penalties for deceit. McMurry had argued that it was the jury who should decide whether or not Scientology was a religion and his closing statement described it as a 'terrorist group' and Hubbard as a sociopath. It was clear that the jury had agreed with him and they had given their verdict on Scientology in no uncertain terms, but there were other factors to be considered. Many fair-minded people felt that the damages were in no way proportionate to the harm suffered by Julie Christofferson. Yet because of a previous ruling by the US Supreme Court it was not possible for the judge to reduce the damages awarded by the jury. A mistrial was the only route open to him to alter the massive sum, but proper grounds had to be shown. Such grounds were readily to hand, since during 1985 the issue of State encroachment upon religious rights had been the subject of considerable controversy in the USA. The Moral Majority had been active in drawing attention to instances such as abortion laws and the teaching of the Creation in schools, in which religion seemed to be losing its guarantees under the Constitution. It was therefore somewhat to the surprise, but delight, of the Scientologists to find themselves getting support from such quarters. The argument had been 'if the Scientologists can be sued today, it might be us tomorrow'.

On Tuesday, 16 July 1985 a breathless court awaited Judge Londer's ruling. First, he rejected objections by the Church of Scientology that jurors had perhaps been influenced prejudicially. He ruled out passion and prejudice as a factor. As the Scientologists' heads sank lower he addressed himself to the question of whether McMurry's closing speech had been improper, prejudicial and had influenced the jury. He continued: 'On the ground that the argument was improper in this court's opinion, that it was prejudicial in this court's opinion — and I can go through, but I don't think there's any necessity to go through and talk about the RPF, the culling of files, all those things that were withdrawn under paragraph XVI and should have come in for one purpose only — the jury considered as a basis for the award of punitive damages. On that basis, given the very substance of being able to say that a court, to any party, is mandated to give a fair trial, there is no other conclusion that this court can reach: on that basis alone, a mistrial must be granted.' The applause from Scientologists within the court-room was deafening. But Judge Londer had one other ground to give them. His directive to the jury that they could determine which Church of Scientology courses were secular and which religious, amounted, he said, to a directed verdict and therefore a mistrial could be granted on that ground. The Scientologists were jubilant. Heber Jentzsch declared that the Church of Scientology was going to use it as a basis to have all the other cases dismissed.

A Church of Scientology advert in the *Oregon State Bar Bulletin* argues: 'If a Catholic prays for rain for his crops and God doesn't answer his prayer, can he then sue the Pope for fraudulent claims? The Pope is God's representative on earth, according to the Catholic religion. Is he therefore not liable to the courts of law? This, far-fetched as it may seem, is precisely the issue which has caused alarm around the country to combat those influences that are systematically eroding the protections of the First Amendment.' The advert, issued after the mistrial decision, continues: 'One's religious beliefs cannot be judged and regulated by the law; one's religion cannot be put on trial. To open the door to this collapse of Church and State is to open the door to the eradication of religious freedom and a veritable religious genocide.' In the post-euphoria of Portland and the rhetoric of freedom under the United States Constitution, it sounds very fine. With a good measure of irony, the Scientologists have now begun to turn the rhetoric of their opponents back into their faces.

My inquisitor from my Los Angeles visit, 'Rev' Ken Hoden, says of the Titchbourne claimant: 'Deprogrammers kidnapped her from the church and held her for five days. She was made into a mindless robot and fired at the church like a bullet. What you're looking at is a set-up.' Hoden is in no doubt that 'IRS operatives' were behind the anti-church campaign. Others had indulged in perjury, he claims, and had broken into church headquarters and stolen documents to use as models for forgeries which would incriminate the church. The huge irony in all these charges is that every one of them mirrors actual crimes proved to have been carried out by the church in the past. It is as if the Church of Scientology has created a shadow and then complained that it is being stalked by it.

The Portland case will be retried and it is likely that particular care will be taken by the attorneys for the plaintiff to satisfy all the legal proprieties. Were it simply a matter of a religious sect on trial for its beliefs then it is likely that Scientology would eventually win public sympathy. But there is ample evidence of criminal wrong-doing by the Church of Scientology in recent years provided by the Guardians' trial and the glut of documents accumulated by Armstrong and evidence given during the case involving him, to suggest that what is at issue is anti-social conduct which no society could tolerate or exempt from legal sanction.

Nevertheless, the church has chalked up two verdicts around the world which it hails as establishing its status as a religion in countries previously hostile to its presence. In AUSTRALIA in October 1983 the High Court considered an appeal by the Church of the New Faith (Scientology's alter ego adopted when it was outlawed in 1965 in Victoria by the Psychological Practices Act). It was brought against the Commissioner for Payroll Tax, claiming tax-exemption as a religion. The Church of Scientology won that action and the judgment included the following sentences: 'Church of Scientology is, for relevant purposes, a religion . . . the adherents accept the tenets of Scientology as relevant to determining their beliefs, their moral standards and their way of life.' Acknowledging that Scientology includes doctrines related to Eastern ones of reincarnation, the court turned its attention to the evidence of less attractive features of Scientology practices. Reference was made to some unusual features of membership and to the strong commercial emphasis in its practices. 'However incongruous or even offensive these features and this emphasis may seem . . . regardless of whether the members of the applicant are gullible or misled or whether the practices of Scientology are harmful or objectionable, the evidence, in our view, establishes that Scientology must, for all relevant purposes, be accepted as "a religion" in Victoria. That does not, of course, mean that the practices of the applicant or its rules are beyond the control of the law of the State or that the applicant or its rules are beyond its taxing powers.' The verdict is a purely legal one and clearly falls short of enthusiastic endorsement. However, the opponents of Scientology in Australia were not slow to hit back. A Select Committee of the South Australia legislature recommended in October 1985 to their parliament in Adelaide that the

Church of Scientology should be monitored for a year so that its financial practices could be assessed. If these were not satisfactory then legislation should be introduced which would strictly control the finances of 'spiritual organizations'. The Church of Scientology protested that this was State interference with religious freedoms and that the Committee had given undue stress in its report to the testimony of seven disaffected Scientologists among the two hundred and forty witnesses they had heard. Legislation is not planned but the report is a significant warning shot across the bows of 'Commodore' Hubbard's Navy that its future in Australia is not likely to be one of live-and-let-live.

In another case heard in GERMANY in June 1985 the District Court of Stuttgart acquitted a Scientology staff member on charges of disseminating his religion as a 'trade'. The judge stated 'the fact that services, activities etc. offered by a religious community are offered against a fee does not justify the conclusion that this constitutes the practice of trading; this at least does not apply when activities stand in direct relationship to the religion itself'. In welcoming the verdict, Heber Jentzsch said that he hoped the US courts and Government agencies would take note of this decision and warned if they did not 'we are for sure headed for a holocaust worse than what took place in Germany'.

In ENGLAND the Church of Scientology took a hammering in the Family Division of the Royal Courts of Justice in London on 23 July 1984. As mentioned in Chapter 1, Mr Justice Latey delivered a judgment in open court on a custody case involving two children. The issue became Scientology and its potentially harmful effect on the children if they were allowed to remain with their father, who was still a practising Scientologist. Dr John Clark came over from Boston to testify. The Scientologists themselves were not legally represented because they were not cited and admitted later they were 'caught napping'.

From the bench Mr Justice Latey delivered one of the most damaging attacks ever mounted in public on the Church of Scientology. He called Hubbard a 'charlatan' and described what he professed as 'a cynical lie'. The Church of Scientology was 'training for slavery' in its effect upon the young. His judgment included within it several HCOBs dealing with the more perfidious practices such as Fair Game, Red Box data, the Guardians' covert activities and training in how to lie. The Guardians' crimes and culling of pc folders were detailed. Justice

Latey declared: 'I have searched and searched carefully for anything good, some redeeming feature, in Scientology. I can find nothing, unless it be such participation as there has been in the drug-abuse campaign.'

The judgment went far further than any previous published attack on the Church of Scientology and was privileged, having been delivered in court. The Fleet Street Press had a field-day and ran headlines picking out adjectives such as 'obnoxious', 'charlatan', 'like Hitler' to run alongside photographs of Hubbard. Whether the motive of the judge was to warn the public about the dangers of Scientology, he succeeded in creating immense adverse publicity for the Church of Scientology. Here is how he concluded:

> 'Scientology is both immoral and socially obnoxious. In my judgment it is corrupt, sinister and dangerous. It is corrupt because it is based on lies and deceit and has as its real objective money and power for Mr Hubbard, his wife and those close to him at the top. It is sinister because it indulges its infamous practices both to its adherents who do not toe the line unquestioningly and to those outside who criticize or oppose it. It is dangerous because it is out to capture people, especially children and impressionable young people, and indoctrinate and brainwash them so that they become the unquestioning captives and tools of the cult, withdrawn from ordinary thought, living, and relationships with others.'

You can't get much more negative than that. It goes without saying that Mr Justice Latey did not award custody of the children to their Scientologist father.

The case resulted in an Appeal Court hearing in September 1984 before Lord Justice Dunn and Lord Justice Purchas with the father being supported by the Church of Scientology, which contended that the issue of Scientology had figured too prominently in the case. The Church supplied a document to me dated 16 October 1984 which purported to be 'a brief summary of the appeal court judgment'. I was somewhat surprised to read that Mr Justice Latey's judgment had apparently been 'inaccurate and unfair' in six respects. He had apparently been seen by the Appeal Court to have gone into unnecessary detail about Scientology, to have erred by giving judgment in open court and breached natural justice by condemning Scientology unheard. However, on going to the actual transcript of the Appeal Court judgment of Wednesday 19 September 1984, I found that it

149

had upheld Justice Latey *in every single respect*. The nearest it came to criticizing him was the following: 'it was, of course, a matter for the ... learned judge whether or not he gave judgment in open court. It was not necessary for him to have done so, and it was unfortunate that he gave as one of his reasons for doing so the protection of the public as well as the other reason, that is to say, the importance of the reasons for his decision being publicly known so as to avoid rumour and speculation. *I cannot say that he was wrong to do so*.' [my italics]

Lord Justice Dunn went on, 'The judge having made the findings which he did about the practice of Scientology, which were not challenged in this appeal and the judge having refused to accept the father's assurances, I can find no ground on which this court could interfere with the judgment and the appeal is dismissed.'

I have quoted this example at length to illustrate the misinterpretation carried on by the Church of Scientology and the unreliability of the so-called documentation which is supplied in rebuttal of charges against it or in order to discredit its adversaries. Whether this is out of sheer stupidity, blind loyalty or wilful falsehood in this instance I cannot tell. But it would appear that to Scientologists, the decision of a court means what they want it to mean.

All the money which the Scientologists are spending worldwide on legal fees is still not stemming the tide. They are being forced into levels of spending in California said to run at $1.5 million per month. The adverse publicity has had its effect on 'stats' and income from fees is not rising to meet this. The haemorrhage in membership with the advent of the independents has also meant less income. On the other hand, cases like Armstrong's have resulted in a flow of new ammunition against the church and verdicts like that of the Portland jury have encouraged the opponents of the Church of Scientology to try their hand in court. The wagons are gathering in a circle. More and more Indians are gathering on the hills and there is no cavalry who look likely to come to the rescue of the beleaguered Scientologists.

Michael Flynn, when I left him, was eagerly looking forward to another case being opened in Toronto, Canada, against the Church of Scientology. Nineteen members and former members face a variety of charges from theft to possession of property obtained by crime and breach of trust. So far the Canadians have moved slowly. But it is whispered that more Guardians' sins will emerge from this trial. It results from the seizure of more than 250,000 documents from the Church of Scientology offices in downtown Toronto in March 1983 as the culmination of a nine-year investigation.

However, the war in the courts has still not resulted in the annihilation of the Church of Scientology. It has cleverly fought back by using the freedom of religion issue as a new battlefield on which its troops take the higher ground of moral philosophy. Hubbard's generals have also turned their fire on a ferocious bear in the shape of the Internal Revenue Service (IRS) in the United States. Week after week *Freedom* magazine rails against the IRS. Infiltration by the Scientologists has only raised the determination of the IRS to bring the Church of Scientology to book. In September 1984 the United States' tax-court in Washington DC ruled that the Californian Church of Scientology was not entitled to a religion's freedom from taxation. The court said that it was operated for the private benefit of founder Hubbard. Though the ruling applies only to the Californian church and the Church of Scientology is appealing, if it stands it will almost certainly be applied by the IRS to all churches of Scientology throughout the USA. That would deal a crippling blow to their finances which would almost certainly put a tourniquet around the life-blood through which Scientology has survived so far — MONEY.

The death of Hubbard will undoubtedly have an effect on many of the lawsuits pending against the Church of Scientology, especially those which name Hubbard personally. In that respect, Hubbard could be said to be more use to his followers dead rather than alive. The bulk of the Portland award was against Hubbard personally and that clearly will not be an option open to future litigants against the church. The RTC will probably do everything in its power to distance the millions it inherited from Hubbard from the predators. It is therefore not on the deranged behaviour of Hubbard, the past crimes of his followers or on the mind-bending effects of the 'tech' upon which the battle will concentrate, but upon the bank accounts and back-taxes which the church can be forced to pay. It is this war of attrition that will eventually kill it off.

The preoccupation with money is documented in the church's Governing Policy formulated in 1972, which begins 'A. MAKE MONEY' and ends with 'MAKE MONEY, MAKE MORE MONEY, MAKE OTHER PEOPLE PRODUCE SO AS TO MAKE MORE MONEY'. Certainly Scientology is not alone in its stress on giving money as a means of grace. There are many forms of religion in the USA, such as some of the preachers of the 'electronic church', who appeal for funds through their programmes, operating on the principle of the medieval indulgence seller, Tetzel, whose jingle was 'as soon as the coin in the coffer rings, the soul from purgatory springs'. He had much in common with Hubbard in his ability to market his religion and make ordinary people think that money could buy them the love of God. But what made Hubbard unique was the fortune, largely tax exempt, which he generated through his book sales and money transferred from Church of Scientology accounts. It made him more than a wealthy preacher or affluent indulgence seller. He was in the tycoon class. Yet what poverty of spirit lurked in the shadow of the millionaire recluse. He founded a religion whose goal was to clear the planet and make people free in spirit and healthy in mind, yet there were few instances of the money being used for philanthropic purposes. It was siphoned off while the social programmes of Scientology (Narconon and the Citizens Commission for Human Rights) were, and still are, run by the slave labour of the org staffers who are paid measly pocket-money and have the RPF hanging over their heads if they dare disobey.

A pincer movement from lawyers and psychiatrists on the one hand and from the IRS on the other to squeeze the Church of Scientology money supply dry, could soon bring about the demise of the monster which Hubbard created in his own image, paranoid and schizophrenic. Its two faces, the young and idealistic recruits and the officer elite of the RTC, represent its disturbed personality. Its paranoid attacks on government and health agencies demonstrate its ultimate destructive nature. As the lawyers and the IRS men close in, the Scientologists may well be justified in saying, 'Just because we're paranoid, it doesn't mean they're not out to get us.' They are!

8 Battlefield Earth

WANTED. DEAD OR ALIVE – L. RON HUBBARD. After 1980 in the Wild Western world of Scientology, with cowboys chasing Indians, goodies and baddies fighting it out at the OK corral of org-speak, Hubbard was a man with a price on his head. Hubbard the science-fiction writer, Hubbard the founder of a religion and its guru and dictator, became Hubbard the recluse. Even his wife did not see or meet him after 1980. His communication lines were limited to the select troika of the Broekers and David Miscavige.

The motives for his going into hiding were obvious. A plethora of lawsuits were being filed against the Church and he was named in several. There was other evidence uncovered which linked him to conspiracies and illegal acts. The possibility grew into a probability that the founder of Scientology would be indicted, faced with the indignity of going on trial in a blaze of publicity and very probably sent to prison. Ron and his followers were determined that this would not happen to him, but he knew that he had accumulated plenty of enemies who were anxious to see him behind bars. That was one overwhelming reason for L. Ron Hubbard to disappear.

As already mentioned, the official reason given for his disappearance was that Hubbard wished to devote himself to writing and research. To support this contention a new blockbuster science-fiction novel entitled *Battlefield Earth* emerged from his seclusion and was published in the USA in October 1982 and immediately shot up the bestseller lists. It was hailed by the triumphant Scientologists as proof that Ron was up there with the best of them, but opponents of Scientology said it was a work of mediocre quality which had only got there because of massive advertising campaigns. Disaffected Scientologists like John Zegel allege that this technique was also used with the promotion of DMSMH, re-launched in 1984 with a television advertising campaign which Zegel says cost over $6 million, and claims twelve books could have been given away free with every one sold and the same income achieved. Such promotions he sees as window-dressing exercises which yield a high public profile. The statistics are then used by the Church of Scientology to claim success.

The story of *Battlefield Earth* is, in Hubbard's words, as follows: 'Mankind has almost been wiped from the face of the Earth by advanced technology and is imprisoned not so much by aliens who dominate the planet, but by superstition, and the few surviving tribes — hiding like frightened animals — have taken to superstition until the hero Johnny Goodboy Tyler decides to leave the mountain sanctuary of his dying tribe and becomes the first to break free of superstition.' But there were those in October 1982 who looked at the Church of Scientology and were convinced that it had been taken over by aliens and that their hero Hubbard was either incapacitated or dead.

In November 1982 Hubbard's estranged son, Ronald DeWolf brought a probate case in Riverside, California, asking that his father be declared dead or mentally incompetent and that the assets of his father's estate be turned over to him. He alleged that Miscavige and Co had staged a coup and had stolen the golden eggs. But the old goose was not beaten yet. As we have seen, Hubbard was able to prove to the satisfaction of Judge J. David Hennigan that he was alive. Judge Hennigan concluded in his judgment of 27 June 1983: 'Mr Hubbard's constitutional right of privacy gives him a right to keep his residence a secret from the public and, therefore, he is not a Missing Person within the meaning of Probate Code 260.'

The circumstances were somewhat bizarre and in keeping with the cloak-and-dagger blanket of security which Hubbard had woven for himself. No official of the court saw him, but a special formula ink was supplied to his agents and this was used to sign an affidavit submitted to the court. It was initialled on each page and Hubbard's thumbprint appended together with a handwritten postscript. These were authenticated by Forensic Document Examiner William L. Bowman and the ink verified to be the same as that supplied. In Hubbard's declaration he described DeWolf's action as 'malicious' and added that not only had his son been disinherited, but would be disinherited in any future wills he might make.

Hubbard continued: 'I am not a missing person. I am in seclusion of my own choosing. My privacy is important to me and I do not wish it or my affairs invaded in the manner permitted by this action. As Thoreau secluded himself by Walden Pond, so I have chosen to do so in my own fashion. I am actively writing, having published *Battlefield Earth*, and my *Space Jazz* album; a projected ten-volume work, *Mission Earth*, is in the pre-publication stage at the moment. I am actively researching and writing as well in connection with the religion of Scientology, as I have over the past decades.' Hubbard went on to state that he was exercising his constitutional right not to appear and that his business affairs were being well managed by Author Services Inc., the Los Angeles based profit-making agency run by Miscavige. He said he was aware of the forged cheque for $2 million (the Tamimi affair) but that he had informed the Bank of New England it was a forgery. Hubbard then went on to deal with the establishment of the RTC in this important document, the rest of which is reproduced in full on pages 179–83:

This is the final testament of Ron Hubbard. I say final because it is the last communication which is universally acknowledged to be authentic. The court declaration could have been typed onto pages upon which Hubbard had put his initials and the text typed afterwards, but the fact still remains that the ink, the fingerprints and the signatures all add up to proof that L. Ron Hubbard was alive on 15 May 1983.

Other communications have come from 'LRH's personal office' since that date, typewritten or telexed, but some have been shown to contain inconsistencies of style or facts which make them suspect. The last personal interview which Hubbard gave to the Press appeared in the *Saturday Evening Post* in 1968. The Church of Scientology recently issued a film interview between Hubbard and the South African broadcaster Tony Hitchman but this turned out to be a re-issued version of an original interview done in black and white in the sixties at Saint Hill and prefaced by a new introduction which Hitchman made for Golden Era studios at Gilman Springs. Photographs of Hubbard in recent years are also in short supply, the ones which are most often seen in org premises are either classics from the *Apollo* days or taken in the mid-seventies at Gilman.

However, Hubbard did give one newspaper interview in February 1983 to the *Rocky Mountain News* of Denver, Colorado. It was not in person. Questions were confined to his career as a science-fiction writer and were submitted in writing, and the replies sent back in writing to reporter Sue Lindsay. The primary purpose of Hubbard in granting the interview was to celebrate fifty years as a science-fiction writer and promote the publication of *Battlefield Earth*, which begins its storyline in Denver. Hubbard is mostly looking back on his career but in one answer he is asked if there are any plans for a movie of the book. Hubbard replies with characteristic immodesty: 'Any writer loves glamour town. I used to sit in my penthouse on Sunset Boulevard and write stories for New York and then go to my office in the studio and have my secretary tell everybody I was in conference while I caught up on my sleep because they couldn't believe anybody could write 136 scenes a day and the Screen Writers' Guild would have killed me. Their quota was eight. I commuted between New York and Hollywood with large amounts of time off for the wide open spaces. But I loved Hollywood — still do. Who doesn't? I've recently written three screenplays and some interest has been expressed in *Battlefield Earth*, so I suppose I'll be right back in Hollywood one of these days and probably on location in the Denver area for *Battlefield Earth* when they film it.'

Assuming that the *Rocky Mountain News* interview is authentic and not another of Ron's 'tall tales', it would appear that Hubbard intended to take some hand in the film realization of his sci-fi novel. That would be very plausible, since he had vaunted himself as a director during his Gilman stint. It would be unthinkable that Hubbard would have stayed away from such an enterprise. It was not as if the control had passed out of Scientology hands. In 1982 St Martin's Press sold 125,000 copies of *Battlefield Earth* at $25 each but Bridge Publications (the profit-making publishing arm of the Church of Scientology) bought back the paperback rights and sold the film rights to Salem Productions, and Ken Annakin, a top-rank director, was slated to make two movies based on the book, which had sold 800,000 paperbacks by March 1985. The British rights were similarly retained by the Scientologists themselves. Why then did Hubbard not emerge, even for a brief moment of glory, to take his bow quickly and vanish before the FBI grabbed him? One possibility is that Ron Hubbard died some time after May 1983 — and before November 1983.

Let us first look at the arguments for Hubbard's being alive after 1983. The original reason for his seclusion still held good after that date — namely, that he was in hiding from the authorities. If he were to appear, albeit fleetingly, then he would heighten the chances of being traced to a hiding-place and subpoened to appear in court in one of the many cases pending against him. Whereas with the RTC as a front he could go on working at his ten-volume project and still be sure that the cash registers were ringing bells for him around the world.

He would be able to keep a low profile and maintain his seclusion. This version allows Hubbard to retain control behind the scenes, masterminding the campaign against the enemies of Scientology through his faithful lieutenants and was believed by Dr John Clark until at least mid 1985.

Another version which Flynn seemed to favour in late 1984 was that Hubbard was alive but completely broken in health. He bases this partly on the testimony in the Armstrong case of Kima Douglas, who was Hubbard's personal medical officer until 1980. She testified that Hubbard nearly died in 1978 when David Mayo came to Gilman to administer to him. Again in 1982 LRH was 'completely bedridden', according to Flynn. There was the stroke he suffered in 1975 in Curaçao and a skin cancer on his face. A man who smoked fifty cigarettes per day, who drove himself throughout his life as Hubbard did, who was obese and who was aged 72 in 1983, would not be likely to be in the best of health. Hubbard the complete invalid would also explain the lack of authentic communications from the Scientology leader and the necessity to conceal from the world the fact that the man who sold the power to triumph over disease and to attain clarity of thought was a diseased geriatric.

Those who do not believe this explanation may point to the cassette 'Ron's Journal 38', which was issued to the troops at the end of 1983. This tape consisted entirely of a message from Hubbard and contained a reference to both the DeWolf probate ruling and to the Australia High Court upholding Scientology as a religion, both of which occurred in 1983. It might therefore be presumed that it is a further piece of evidence that Hubbard was alive after 1983, IF IT IS GENUINE. John Zegel, one of the most influential disaffected Scientologists, sent a copy of 'RJ 38' (as the tape is known) plus 'RJ 36' and an earlier Hubbard tape on study methods, to two university departments, one in Canada and one in the USA, who were involved in the analysis of the Watergate tapes. Both sets of experts reported separately that in their opinion the three tapes were made by three separate people and that one of the voices belonged to someone who had spent the early part of his life in California before moving north. Another report, published in the Phoenix journal of an independent Scientology group, declared: 'a voice-print has been done and the results prove that LRH is not the speaker on the last two "Ron's Journals". R. L. Addison of Carson Investigations, Vancouver BC, did the test.' There were reports circulating among the disaffected Scientologists that a voice synthesizer was being used to compile the 'Ron's Journals'.

Rumours also circulated that Ron had been seen in South California. 'They (the RTC) hired a double, a man called Ellis, and he used to pop up in places until the end of 1984,' says Neville Chamberlain who still adheres to the 'tech' in his practice in West Hampstead but is a 'Suppressive Person', having been found guilty of various 'crimes and high crimes' by the Church of Scientology. He is a large man in his forties who was an original Sea Org member way back in the early days. His tough macho image is reinforced by videos of Clint Eastwood, Rollerball and Rocky stacked on a shelf. His black beard bristles as he talks about the RTC, about whom he is bitter. 'I was a front man touring the world, selling the tech. I spoke my mind and was declared SP more often than anyone I know. But I got results. I set up the first centre in Scotland.'

Like many of the independents, Chamberlain is reluctant to see Hubbard as the source of the present troubles but he is realistic about the founder, calling him bluntly 'Hubbard' and not by the affectionate 'LRH' or the respectful 'Mr Hubbard'. 'The technology is basically sound. Hubbard had the perception to put it down. He had a lot of compassion. I've seen him in the depths of despair and apathy. But he was a showman and the next minute he'd be petulant, then Commodore and king of the world. I often thought he ought to have a teeshirt with the words "I'm a schizophrenic — so am I",' quips Chamberlain who is scathing about the effect of the RTC upon the credibility of Scientology. He calls the Guardians the 'Clouseau squad, the blind leading the lame', and argues that the 'Bay of Pigs' which befell Scientology has largely been self-inflicted. He is quite down-to-earth about Scientology's status as a religion. 'I used to wear a dog-collar — what a joke! We used that as a defence-mechanism and a means of tax avoidance.' Like many of the independents who remain loyal to the 'tech' he is convinced that Hubbard would not sanction what is being done by Miscavige.

So was Hubbard aware of what was going on after 1982? If Hubbard was dead, the implications are serious, for that would mean the RTC had perpetrated fraud. But there are other explanations: for instance, that Hubbard was temporarily or permanently incapacitated.

They might also explain why such a large ego as Hubbard's stayed out of the limelight for so long. He might be forgiven for hiding from the mass media who would be likely to ask some hostile questions, but why did he continue to speak to his followers through tape recordings and not through the more effective and personal medium of film or video? The answer which suggests itself to me is that video is far more difficult to forge than sound recording. Hubbard was supposedly devoted to the latest in technical breakthroughs and yet he passed up this opportunity.

There is also the lack of corroboration for his idyllic life at Creston Ranch, San Luis Obispo. It is said he was recognized when he went downtown. Where are the witnesses? Where are the photographs of him tending his orchids, or other pictures which would be a natural by-product of his hobby of photography? Where are the staff who worked with him at the ranch, unless we are asked to believe that a man used to having hordes running around at his every whim suddenly learned the art of cooking and fending for himself. The official Scientology view asks us to believe that Hubbard evaded the FBI, the IRS, the newshounds of the mass media and left no traces of his life as a recluse. If he *did*, then it is strange that no evidence has been produced. The rush to cremate his body and scatter the ashes before an announcement was made arouses even more suspicion among the doubters. I was offered a newspaper cutting by the church, which described a local newspaperman's visit to Creston as 'evidence' of what LRH had been doing for the past six years, yet the reporter was not even permitted to see Hubbard's private quarters or anything that resembled proof that he had indeed lived there. No credible witnesses have emerged to prove that Hubbard was indeed alive and/or well at the ranch. It is difficult to see what purpose would be served by the Scientologists encouraging speculation that Hubbard died long before 1986. If they have proof that he *was* living on his ranch until the official announcement of his death, then it is indeed strange that they do not produce it — unless, of course, the doubters are right and he *did* die in 1983.

Perhaps one day the mystery of those years 1980–86 will be solved. Someone may come forward to give evidence about the final years of the guru's life. Meanwhile, speculation continues that during that period he was increasingly eccentric, wildly paranoid and probably even senile. The more sensational charge — that Hubbard died in 1983 and that his death was covered up — is still believed by many. If true, it would mean that the leadership of the RTC was guilty of deception, conspiracy and fraud. Those who believe this version are faced with explaining how the cabal who headed Scientology managed to pass off the body cremated at San Luis Obispo in 1986 as Hubbard's. Was it a 'stand-in' that they produced for the occasion while supplying some old fingerprints and blood samples of the same group as Hubbard's?

Or was it Hubbard himself who became a corpse in 1983, and was refrigerated and kept on ice for the three years which the troika needed to consolidate their hold on power and to ensure that they had effective control of the church finances?

Such questions are answered by dark mutterings in the homes of breakaway Scientology groups, who accuse Miscavige and Co of stopping at nothing to keep their power. But now that Ron is 'officially' dead, and his ashes scattered over the Pacific Ocean, it will be more difficult to prove matters either way. If Hubbard had indeed died in late 1983 then it would have come at an awkward moment for the RTC. The movement was badly split. It needed to demonstrate that it had Ron's endorsement. It needed the money to finance its policies, which the use of Ron's trademarks gave it. It needed Ron alive and, by whatever means, he stayed that way until it had established its supremacy over Scientology worldwide and its claim to the fortune which he bequeathed it in his will. But it was noticeable that although Ron was 'alive', he certainly was not running the show.

For example, the style of HCOBs altered after Hubbard went into seclusion. It was widely accepted, even by Scientologists, that he was not the author of many of them. His personal control and domination of his organization was very much a feature of Scientology until 1980. But the transcript of the Mission Holders' Conference in 1982 reveals very few references to LRH or his words. It was the same on 21 October 1984 in Clearwater when the Mission holders came together to be addressed by the bigwigs of the RTC. It was Scientology's version of the May Day Parade in Moscow — it would be possible to tell the rising stars in the Politburo by those who were chosen to address the exultant throng and the direction in which Scientology was headed by what they said.

The dominant theme was 'us' against 'them'. 'They' were the IRS, the FBI, the Justice Department, etc. 'The State used to feed us to the lions, now it's to the bureaucrats,' jibed one speaker. 'I'd take the lions — at least you can reason with a lion!' The atmosphere was heady and hysterical, which suited the demagogery of Norman Starkey, the wild recruiting sergeant, who bellowed, 'The first step is, you can join the staff. Get those goddam fence-sitters off the fence and on this side! Contact! Handle! Help by exposing psychiatrists and their horrible product — government!' It was a mixture of an evangelical crusade and an auction sale as Starkey badgered the captive audience into signing a form for a life-time pledge costing

$2,000. 'Hold it up if you're gonna sign. Sign it right now.' Then he snarled, 'What's the deal — some aren't signing it? Life is $2,000!' A woman squealed her assent. Pledges came thick and fast, in a hysterical torrent of bids. One man pledged on behalf of his wife and children who were not there. A black man (a rare sight within the predominantly WASP Church of Scientology) declared to loud applause, 'This is the only game that offers equal opportunity.'

The 'stars' above this firmament were Miscavige who compered the event, Heber Jentzsch, Marc Yaeger (John Zegel's stepson) — CO CMO International — who gave statistics of the latest upsurge in sales of DMSMH but significantly omitted to say much about income from courses, which was reputedly in severe downturn. There was little talk of Hubbard until the end when Commander Vicki Aznaran, a svelte lady of around forty, wearing a silver dress with a plunging neckline, took the stage. In her Texas drawl she talked of building a group 'who knows who its friends and its enemies are . . . there is no question of losing this case 'cos Scientologists never quit. . . . As LRH said in Philadelphia lecture tape 46: "There is no such thing as failure".' Onto the screen of the video-recording I was watching at Saint Hill flashed the face of Hubbard. It could have been my imagination, but the 'feel' of the whole event was that Hubbard was not temporarily absent but had moved on permanently and a new era had begun.

That feeling was reinforced when I sat down to watch the next video. It was portentously titled 'The Religious Freedom Convention' — Earth, 7th October 1984'. It was a very Star Trek, very American, very maudlin parody of the signing of the Declaration of Independence. It contains such phrases as: 'Scientology is experiencing the greatest expansion and prosperity in its history. International in scope, Scientology each week frees more people from the debilitating effects of drugs ignorance and other sources of aberration and moves them on the path to greater awareness, self-respect and dignity than all other groups combined.'

As Heber Jentzsch read the words on the video, gentle music stole up underneath. The ceremony ended with three cheers for 'LRH' as the assembled top brass of the Church of Scientology turned to applaud a large portrait of Hubbard hanging on the wall at Saint Hill where the ceremony was taking place. The camera closed in on the portrait and Hubbard's voice filled the screen. 'In all the broad universe there is no other hope for man than ourselves. This is a tremendous responsibility . . . I have borne it myself too long alone

. . . You share it with me now . . .' The words were from the 1967 Hubbard edition of 'Ron's Journal' but they suddenly had a terrible relevance as to whether or not he was dead. The year was 1984. The year of Big Brother — and the year the little brothers took over.

Epilogue

M UCH has been written so far about the quality of Scientology as a religion. It is worth considering briefly the quantitative side of things. For instance, how many Scientologists are there? As with everything else about this controversial cult the answer is vehemently disputed. Official church statistics were supplied to me for the year 1980 (I asked for a current picture in 1984 but was given this set of figures which pre-dated the 1982–3 split and stats crash). These claim 86 churches, 173 missions, 230 Dianetics groups in 32 countries around the world. They add this up to 5 million Scientologists worldwide and claim 2,500 every week starting a Scientology course, with $25 million invested during 1979–80 in new church quarters in England, Australia, Canada and the USA. There were, on the social reform front, 49 chapters of the Citizens Commission on Human Rights, the anti-psychiatry group and 25 Narconon drug rehabilitation programmes. It looks impressive.

The British membership figure for 1977 in the book *What is Scientology?* was given as 336,000 and the world total as 5,437,000. However, in the *Daily Telegraph* of 28 February 1979, a Church of Scientology official gave the British membership figure as 236,000, and in 1984 church officials talked blithely about 200,000 in the UK. Jon Atack, who has become an archivist of Scientology as well as an antagonist from the independent movement with his journal *Reconnection*, wrote in October 1984: 'Recently I talked with a man who was a senior executive in the UK in 1981. He had access to some of the REAL figures at that time. 5,500 British residents had taken an HQS[1] or above or received paid auditing. That was the total training

[1] Hubbard Qualified Scientologist

and processing list for the entire UK since records were started in the fifties. The total training and processing including non-residents (remembering that Saint Hill was the centre of the Scientology world from 1959–68) was 16,000 and the total central file figure for the UK was 57,000', which would include someone who had bought a small booklet or put down a ten-pence deposit to escape from the Registrar. In 1981 a Hubbard document (LRH ED 326 INT) issued on 13 March 1981 declared: 'I am told that there are TWO MILLION Scientologists active around the world today.' The wild divergence between these figures can only be explained as a mixture of lies and bluff or a different method of accounting for members. If everyone who has walked through the door of an org or taken a personality test is counted, then the five million may be nearer the mark. But one then has to add that many take the test as a joke or never follow it up. In Scotland I know of two people who got onto a Scientology mailing-list yet had expressed no interest at all and for years received regular unsolicited mail almost weekly. Both tried to have this dripping tap stopped but letters to Hubbard and a lawyer's letter failed to staunch the flow. Both persons had titled parents which may explain something about the target area of Scientology recruitment. But whether or not the Church of Scientology was operating a 'quality' recruitment policy, its phenomenal income from such small statistics tempts one to say never mind the quantity, feel the depth of commitment.

High price levels also had something to do with the high income of the Church of Scientology. Although the price of a 'bible' (DMSMH) was £3.50 in paperback in high-street bookshops in the UK in 1984, the price of the same book in hardback at the local org was £40.85. (To be fair, the org also sell the paperback but there is pride taken in buying the best edition available.) I bought 'Ron's Journal 38' in January 1983 at Saint Hill and was charged over £16 for a 30-min. speech cassette. The Philadelphia Doctorate cassettes of Hubbard's lecture-tour in December 1952 are more expensive. Originally delivered over 18 days, these 62 lectures on cassette cost $2,307 for the boxed set. At that rate they are antiques. Auditing prices are the luxury end of the market and in 1984 went up by 10% in July. Here are a few examples prevailing in September 1984 when I called at 'Flag' in Clearwater, which offers the most expensive part of the 'Bridge': Student Hat, $1,610; 'New Era Dianetics' course, $2,290. (These are the two courses for which 'Alyson' paid over £6,000 in 1980–81, which is roughly $8,000. Using her, a graduate, as a guide we can deduce that the actual cost to complete the courses with the extra auditing required would be roughly four times the advertised prices.) To become a Class VII Auditor cost $9,012. Twelve hours regular auditing was $2,765. Twelve hours 'Confessional' was the same — $2,765. But the steepest slope was for thetans: OT I ($648); OT II ($2,222); OT III ($5,774). We may thus assume that the price of climbing to the 'heaven' of OT III in the Kingdom of Hubbard was a minimum of $10,000. There was little chance of those who reached it having laid up treasures on earth where moth and rust could corrupt them. They would have spent them trying to get there.

Every Scientologist is required to show evidence of productivity. These 'stats' are used as a measure of performance, much as salesmen are given sales targets to meet. As everyone knows, a good salesman can sell a rotten product and in selling techniques the Church of Scientology has been one of the most successful new religious movements, or cults, of recent years. The Moonies are identified with selling on street corners, the Hare Krishna devotee with chanting in skimpy robes on chilly winter mornings, the Rajneeshee with free love on a campus, all these activities being somewhat offputting to the man on the Clapham omnibus. But the fresh young man from Scientology with his double-glazed eyes and cavity-foam insulated emotions, identifies much more with the values of Western consumer society. He offers a unique but apparently still marketable product — spiritual advancement (the one thing the suburban young man who has everything feels he lacks). Ron Hubbard could not have made all those millions if he did not have a very effective selling technique. Many of the critics of Scientology are reluctant to admit even this grudging compliment to Scientology's effectiveness. But company profits are not an endorsement of the quality of the product. If the 'product' analogy is continued it can also be seen that Scientology has not had mass appeal. It goes for a particular target consumer, one might even say the top end of the market in financial terms. The young middle-class business or professional person is the typical purchaser. Staff members are often recruited much younger than this. One young man I spoke to claimed to have been in charge of personnel records at Saint Hill at the grand old age of fourteen. That illustrates another facet of Scientology, the ease of promotion within the staff. The young ambitious person can rise quickly within the ranks to positions of power. This facet of Scientology satisfies both the thrusting young businessman type and the quester after spiritual truth. Both wish to feel that they have something (a product/esoteric knowledge) beyond the reach of the man in the street. Instead of climbing the ladder of the rat race, there is a ready-made gnostic ladder and all that is needed is money. With other religions, social background or moral imperfection may count against one. The divorcee may not be able to take Mass, but in Scientology the only sin is ignorance (or perhaps inability to pay for courses). Any club likes to feel that its membership is 'special' and the Church of Scientology is no different. Outsiders are referred to as 'wogs' or 'raw meat'. This attitude was typified for me when I called at the New York City premises of Scientology and met Kevin Brown, the 35-year-old Director of Public Affairs. Educated at a prestigious Jesuit school, he was not slow to point out he had carried off various glittering prizes and had held down a hot-shot job at ABC TV before joining the Scientology staff. He now earns $30 per week plus commission on the copies of DMSMH, which is being pushed hard on the streets of New York by the org. He had worked on the streets himself for six years of the eight since he joined the staff, and acts and talks like a businessman on his way to the top. He became disillusioned with television as a career, regarding it as 'junk food' for the mind, and over-influenced by programme advisers who shared the outlook of psychiatry. 'Nothing in the world was going to change as a result of my doing that job. It lacked the technology,' he announced. 'I felt with all my background and experience that this subject needed the best and finest — and I was going to supply some of it. If people are alert and bright enough they will see that this planet is threatened with total annihilation. If people value the material universe more than Scientology then they are gonna have problems. We're not saying that material possibilities are bad — but don't let it interfere with Scientology. Its most effective method is to train people to receive and deliver. You can go a long way on not a lot if you go that route.'

These young highwaymen of the streets who stand and deliver the 'tech' are not short on dedication. In this they resemble many of the other religious cults which have arisen in Western society since the sixties. But when dedication is transmuted into fanaticism then problems are bound to arise. In a long letter describing his disillusion-ment with the Church of Scientology, a Los Angeles designer, Bruce Bishop, puts the moment of his break eloquently: 'I attended a meeting in which an intelligent CMO Executive named Brian Anderson, stated with righteous fervour that the tech is senior to the law, senior to the Bill of Rights . . . until then I had been unable to understand how these fellows could justify their actions, how they could find the concept of fundamental rights ludicrous. Now it became clear to me. These guys honestly believe they are above the law. "God is on our side. We can do no wrong, for ours is the true faith. Any means are justified by our lofty end." This is the primrose path that led a number of our executives into prison.'

But the flaws in Scientology as a religion are far more fundamental than using the wrong means to achieve its declared aim of a world free from insanity, crime and nuclear war. Nor is its greed for money the root of its evil, for money is essentially morally neutral. It is my contention that Scientology is not so much misplaced idealism or corrupt practices, as inevitably and logically a system which contains the seeds of its own suppression and destruction. In Scientology, it is a fundamental postulate that any handicap to spiritual advancement is caused by engrams (incidents in the reactive mind which can be E-Metered out. This leads logically to the position that all past deeds and misdeeds can be managed by a process or technique and are therefore not moral or immoral — they are amoral. Scientology is religion without morality, since moral improvement is not derived from an outside source or power (spirit, grace, brahmin, karma etc). At first sight it resembles some of the Free Spirit heresies of the 14th century or the Anabaptists of the 16th century. But Scientology's Revelation is not from a divine source, it is the product of Hubbard's mind and personality. Therefore it inherits the flaws and characteristics of that personality, which we have amply demonstrated is self-seeking, paranoid and vindictive. It should therefore come as no surprise that the collective mind and system of Scientology is in essence paranoid and challenging to moral systems and forms of authority. It is truly suppressive in reacting to moral claims upon it. Since it does not acknowledge a source of meaning, morality or revelation superior to the tech, it resists these claims upon the amoral basis of strength and power. There is no appeal to higher authority — God, the law, human rights — when disputing with Ron and his men, for they have opted to be outside the moral assumptions upon which all these concepts are grounded. Thus in their struggles with governments, law, medicine, the media, they have become truly subversive. In so doing they effectively challenge Society to control them or be undermined. This is *not* a battle for the freedom of religion, with the State on one side and Scientology on the other . . . It is a choice between freedom, as we know it, and *anarchy*. The Gotterdämmerung for Scientology has arrived with the death of the god-hero Hubbard but it was not governments or the taxmen or the lawyers or psychiatrists who lit the funeral pyre but the inflammatory nature of his own ideas. He was, according to the term he defined himself, a truly 'Suppressive Person'.

Appendices

Org Board of International Management

?
|
Ann & Pat Broeker
|
David Miscavige
|

Religious Technology Center	Author Services Incorporated
	(A profit-making corporation)
	Bridge Publications
	Church Legal
	Church Finance
	Church Corporate Affairs
Church of Scientology International	Marketing
Watchdog Committee	
Commodore's Messenger Organization	International Finance Police
Executive Director International	
Executive Strata	
International Management Organization	
Flag Operations Liaison Offices	Scientology Missions International

'He who holds the power of an organization is that person who holds its communication lines and who is a crossroad of the communications.'
(*How to Live Though an Executive*. L. Ron Hubbard)

TRANSLATION

Irmgard Wassard
Examined graphologist
Member of the Danish Graphologist Society

26.3.1984

Declaration

concerning possible authenticity/spuriousness of signature by L. Ron Hubbard.

Material:- 2 doubtful signatures (photostatic copies) marked X and Y by me.

Material for comparison:- 2 original signatures marked H by me.

The examination of the above written material has led to the following result:-

The two doubtful signatures show so much mutual similarity in the writing movement and the shape of the letters, in the breaking-off of lines, the tilt, and not least in the chaos of big loops in the upper zone of the writing that there is

   a probability amounting almost to certainty

a) that the two signatures have been made by the same person and
b) that that person is not identical with the person (L. Ron Hubbard) who has signed his name on the appendices marked H, since the doubtful signatures show a multitude of deviations from the authentic writing which are typical of forgeries.

The result of the examination is based on the following observations:-

1. App. H: The writing movement is elastic
   - XY: The writing movement is unelastic

2. App. H: The lines are predominantly unbroken
   - XY: The lines are markedly broken (break-offs, holes)

3. App. H: The letters "ubbard" are clearly shaped and easily legible
   - XY: The letters "ubbard" are unclearly shaped and partly difficult to read.

Irmgard Wassard   2.

4. App. H: 3 separate loops in the upper zone
   - XY: Only 2 loops in the upper zone + extra lines which cross the loops
     so that the whole upper zone becomes an entangled, overdimensioned
     chaos whereas the same zone is clear to read in the authentic sig-
     natures.

5. App. H: The top loop of the H points upwards and bends slightly to the right
   - XY: The top loop of the H is lying like an eiderdown on top of almost
     all of the last name.

6. App. H: There is great distance from the said right loop of the H to the
     top of the d, the leftwards movement of which forms an angle with
     the finishing line which points to the right.
   - XY: The loop of the H and the top part of the "d" are entangled.

7. App. H: The change of writing direction in the top part of the "d" makes
     an acute angle.
   - XY: The change of writing direction in the top part of the "d" forms
     an oval bow.

8. App. H: The letter d is written in one unbroken movement
   - XY: In app. X the upstroke has been added later, and in fact in the
     wrong place. - In app. Y the upstroke has no connection with the
     basic curve.

9. App. H: The letters "bb" are written in an unbroken movement
   - XY: The letters "bb" are separate; one b is illegible in App. X.

10. App. H: The b's have a very short upper part.
    - XY: The b's have a very long, towering upper part which either touches
      or crosses the transverse loop from the letter "H".

11. App. H: From basis to top the b's are 8-9 mm high
    - XY: From basis to top the b's are 15, 17, and 19 mm high, respectively.

12. App. H: The letter "u" is written in an unbroken movement with the letters
      H and b
    - XY: The letter "u" is completely isolated.

13. App. H: The angle of tilt in the b's is 58°
    - XY: The angle of tilt is the b's is 35 and 45°, respectively.

Irmgard Wassard   3.

14. App. H: The angle of tilt of the "n" is 130° to the left
    - XY: The angle of tilt of the "n" is 60° to the right.

15. App. H: The upper and lower loops of the letter "l" are 10 and 9 mm long,
            respectively
    - XY: The upper loops are 30 and 32 mm, respectively
          The lower loop is but a small, narrow crossing to two lines.

16. App. H: A cross section of the upper loop of the "H" measures 2 and 3 mm,
            respectively
    - X: A cross section of the upper loop of the "H" is 3 mm
    - Y: A cross section of. the upper loop of the "H" is 9 mm.

17. App.XY: The letter L contains an extra line in the first, lower convexity
            which is parallel to the overlying line and the initial line of
            the L.
    - Y: contains the same line in a shorter version within the convexity.
         Furthermore this line is broken off at both ends and has the same
         hook to the right on its top part.
    - H: Nothing similar is found in App. H.

18. App. H: In the letter L there is great distance between the rightwards
            initial upstroke and the lower upstroke from the bottom loop,
            viz. 7 mm.
    - XY: The same distance has been measured to 4 and 1 mm, respectively.

19.   Apart from all this, there are so many interruptions of the writing,
            interruptions of the line, added lines, irrelevant additions,
            omissions and failing imitations (marked by me with little red
            arrows) that the conclusion must be that there is
            a probability amounting almost to certainty that the signatures
            on the appendices X and Y are forgeries of the signature of
            L. Ron Hubbard.

N.B.   The phrase "a probability amounting almost to certainty" is the
            strongest phrase used in cases of this nature, also by the police.

            It is my personal, honest belief that the doubtful signatures are
            not authentic.

                                    (Sign. I. Wassard)

I the undersigned Lisbet Pals Svendsen, official translator, hereby certify the foregoing text to be a true and faithful translation of the attached photostatic copy of declaration from Ms. I. Wassard in the Danish language produced to me this 28th day of March, 1984.
It should be noted that the appendices marked H, X and Y have not been translated by me, but were handed to me along with the other material.

Witness my hand and official seal.

Lisbet Pals Svendsen
Official translator and interpreter.

b.   RTC hereby indemnifies LRH and agrees to hold him harmless from and against all liabilities, claims and actions of any kind, and costs, including attorneys' fees, which relate to the Marks or services in connection with which they are used.

Signed in duplicate at Los Angeles, California on the date first above written.

L. Lafayette Ronald Hubbard

HÅNDBOG I DIANETIKKENS METODE

Dianetik

DEN MODERNE VIDENSKAB OM MENTAL SUNDHED

L. Ron Hubbard

NOW, THEREFORE, for good and valuable consideration, the receipt of which is hereby acknowledged, said L. Ron Hubbard does hereby assign unto said Religious Technology Center all of his rights, title and interest in and to the above-identified marks, registrations and applications for registrations, together with all goodwill symbolized by the marks.

Date: /5 June . 19

L. RON HUBBARD

IN WITNESS WHEREOF, I have hereunto set my hand and affixed by official seal, the day and year in this certificate first above written.

Notary Public in and for said
County and State

L·S

OFFICIAL SEAL
DAVID MISCAVIGE
NOTARY PUBLIC · CALIFORNIA
LOS ANGELES COUNTY
My comm. expires JAN 11, 1985

APPENDIX C

SUPERIOR COURT OF THE STATE OF CALIFORNIA

FOR THE COUNTY OF RIVERSIDE

In Re Estate of)   CASE NO. 47150
)
    L. RON HUBBARD,   )   (Probate)
)
    A Missing Person.   )   STATEMENT OF DECISION
)
_____)

The court makes the following Statement of Decision:

The declaration of L. RON HUBBARD, dated May 15, 1983, is in Mr. Hubbard's handwriting with his fingerprint attached, and was executed after this action began.

The lack of information as to Mr. Hubbard's present residence address is a matter of choice by Mr. Hubbard.

Mr. Hubbard's business affairs are being taken care of to the satisfaction of Mr. Hubbard, and are not in need of supervision by this court.

Mr. Hubbard's constitutional right of privacy gives him a right to keep his residence a secret from the public and, therefore, he is not a Missing Person within the meaning of Probate Code 260.

Dated: June 27, 1983   J. DAVID HENNIGAN
                                    _____
                                    J. DAVID HENNIGAN
                                    JUDGE OF THE SUPERIOR COURT

DECLARATION OF L. RON HUBBARD

I, L. RON HUBBARD, declare and say:

1. I am the L. Ron Hubbard who is the subject of this action, entitled In re the Estate of L. Ron Hubbard, No. 47150. Although I have not appeared in this matter, and do not intend to do so, as I shall explain further on in this declaration, I am nevertheless familiar with this proceeding.

2. I am submitting this declaration because I have been informed that the court in this case has indicated that it may not accept a letter sent by me to it, dated 3 February 1983, but may be willing to accept a sworn state-ment from me. I am thus submitting this sworn declaration in a further effort on my part to put an end to this matter, although I do not frankly believe that there is any basis for this action even without my declaration. As with my previous letter, I am offering my fingerprint on each page of this declaration.

3. I am aware of this action, and I am aware that the basis of it is that my eldest son, Ronald DeWolf, from whom I have been estranged for over twenty years, contends that I am a missing person whose estate is in need of attention, supervision and care. I am further aware that he claims my health is bad, that I am not competent to handle my affairs, that I may be held prisoner against my will, and that my estate is being dissipated by Scientologists. All of this is totally false, malicious and ill-founded, as I will elaborate.

4. With respect to Ronald DeWolf, I consider him neither a friend nor a family member in the true sense of the word. Although biologically he is my son, his hostility and animosity to me are apparent and have been for years. While I consider this an unfortunate situation, it is none-theless a fact. I have disinherited him by name in the various wills I have prepared over the past many years; he is disinherited in my current will; and I intend to disin-herit him in any future wills. In this regard, I do not wish to have turned over to the court or DeWolf my present will and inter-vivos trust as I consider them personal, private, and privileged documents, which are subject to disclosure only at the time of death. But I do think it is relevant that the court be aware that Ronald DeWolf is disinherited.

5. I am not a missing person. I am in seclusion of my own choosing. My privacy is important to me, and I do not wish it or my affairs invaded in the manner permitted by this action. As Thoreau secluded himself by Walden Pond, so I have chosen to do so in my own fashion. I am actively writing, having published Battlefield Earth, and my Space Jazz album; a projected ten volume work, Mission Earth, is in the pre-publication stage at the moment. I am actively researching and writing as well in connection with the religion of Scientology, as I have over the past decades.

6. I do not intend to appear in this action as doing so would constitute a violation of my right to privacy, a

2

1. right which is precious to me and which is protected by the
2. United States and California Constitutions. For the same
3. reasons, I do not choose to appear for any deposition as, I
4. am informed, this court has suggested I do.

5. 7. My affairs are not in need of attention,
6. supervision and care. My business manager, Author Services,
7. Inc.; does a good job at handling my affairs, and I retain
8. complete control on all important matters, including signing
9. my own checks and receiving detailed and regular reports. I
10. believe that Mr. Lyman Spurlock, of Author Services, Inc.,
11. has explained this to the court. I have a fine battery of
12. expert professionals who advise me as well. I believe that
13. Mr. Spurlock and Sherman Lenske, an attorney who represents
14. me in various business and financial affairs, have also
15. explained this to the court. I meet all of my obligations,
16. including tax obligations; support my wife; supervise my
17. investments; and do all the other things attendant upon a
18. responsible person's handling of his affairs.

19. 8. Specifically, with respect to the allegations of
20. mismanagement of my affairs contained in the DeWolf peti-
21. tion, I am aware of the circumstances of each. The
22. allegations are false. There was an effort to pass a large
23. forged check on my E. F. Hutton account in June, 1982, but
24. it was those at Author Services who immediately ensured that
25. it not be cashed and informed me; as a result, I wrote the
26. Bank of New England and advised it that the check was not
27. from me. The gems allegation is also false. Jim Isaacson
28.

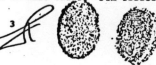

3

1 did, at my direction, attempt to sell a small stone in the
2 summer of 1982, although he was not successful. I bought
3 some stones through Intercap, Ltd., around that same time.
4 These stones are in my possession and their purchase was
5 approved by me. I have transferred my religious trademarks
6 to the Religious Technology Center, but I retain full owner-
7 ship of any commercial applications of the marks as well as
8 full ownership of all my copyrights and patent rights, none
9 of which have been transferred. Contrary to the uninformed
10 allegations of the petition, my trademark transfer involved
11 no monetary loss. Finally, I and only I sign my name on any
12 of my accounts or contract documents, etc. There is no
13 truth to the allegation that anyone else signs my checks or
14 other financial documents using my name.
15   9. My health is fine. Of course, I am older now than
16 I used to be, but age comes to us all. In my case, I am
17 fortunate to be in good health and thus able to maintain my
18 heavy daily work schedule. As to the claim of my incompe-
19 tence, I do not intend to dignify it with a response. My
20 life, my work, my activities, my publications, and my con-
21 tinuing handling of my affairs speak for themselves.
22 Similarly, the absurd charge that I am being held prisoner
23 is not worthy of response. Anyone who knows me knows how
24 ridiculous such an idea is. Equally ridiculous is the idea
25 that Scientologists would steal from me. Scientology is
26 based upon the research, study and writing I have done over
27 a lifetime, work I continue to this day. Scientologists ar
28

1 my most trusted associates and would never do anything to
2 harm me, much less hold me prisoner or steal from me.

3   10. Since there apparently have been specific
4 allegations of wrongdoing by David Miscavige, I wish to take
5 this opportunity to communicate my unequivocal confidence in
6 David Miscavige, who is a long time devoted Scientologist, a
7 trusted associate, and a good friend to me. Any activities
8 which he may have engaged in at any time concerning my per-
9 sonal or business affairs have been done with my knowledge
10 and authorization and for my benefit. The charges that he
11 is organizing the theft of my assets are completely false
12 and not worthy of further comment than that.

13   11. Due to my concern for my own privacy, and also due
14 to my concern for my personal security (there have been
15 numerous threats against my life over the years), I have
16 always kept my residence a complete secret or one known only
17 to a few close confidants.

18   12. I realize that, to the court, my refusal to come
19 forward may appear unusual. However, be that as it may, it
20 is my choice and my right. As I explained in my earlier
21 letter, I find this the most satisfactory way at present of
22 avoiding the hurly burly of distracting things.

23   13. I am aware that my dear wife of over thirty years,
24 Mary Sue, has appeared in this action to oppose this effort
25 to appoint a trustee over my estate. I support her in this
26 effort and am submitting this declaration in the hope and
27 expectation that her position will be rapidly vindicated.

28

5

181

1 Although we are presently apart, we remain husband and wife.

2 She is fully supported by me, and she, unlike DeWolf, is

3 fully provided for in my will.

4   14. I have not wanted to repeat all the matters which

5 I recited in my earlier letter to this court, dated

6 February 3, 1983, but by this reference I incorporate them

7 as if fully set forth herein.

8   15. I have personal knowledge of all the matters set

9 forth above and am competent to testify to them.

10   16. I respectfully request that this action now be

11 terminated once and for all. I believe that it is brought

12 maliciously, in bad-faith, and certainly for motives other

13 than protecting me, my estate or my heirs.

14   17. I will handwrite out the final portion of this

15 declaration, which recites that it is sworn to under the

16 laws of the State of California, in addition to the typed

17 version, so that there will be ample handwriting with which

18 to conduct a handwriting analysis.

19   I declare, under penalty of perjury and under the laws

20 of the State of California, that the foregoing is true and

21 correct.

22

23 Dated:

24 15 May 83

25

26

27

28

3F:DWLF:VI:DCL:LRH

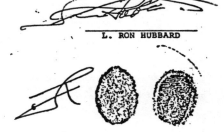

L. RON HUBBARD

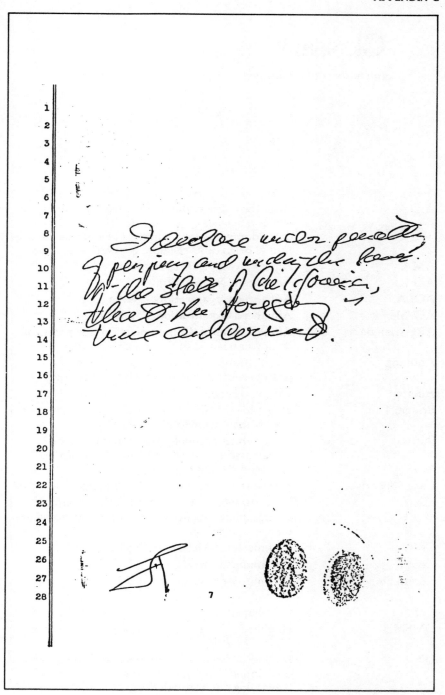

Glossary

(including abbreviations)

A.D.	After the publication of Hubbard's *Dianetics: the Modern Science of Mental Health* in 1950, the date adopted by the Church of Scientology as the *fons et origo* of its religion. So 1986 = A.D.36
AMA	American Medical Association
AO	Advanced Organization
AOLA	Advanced Organization, Los Angeles
AO/SH	Advanced Organization/Saint Hill
ARC triangle	Affinity, Reality, Communication (the points of the lower triangle of the church's symbol)
Auditing	Application of Scientology processes and procedures to someone by a trained auditor.
Auditor	One who listens: person who trains preclears
Bridge, The	Stepladder of courses undertaken by students of Scientology, from grades I to XII.
Buttons	Areas which produce a reaction (of pain or embarrassment) in the student which need to be 'flattened' by auditing processes.
Case Supervisor	Someone who supervises the auditing of preclears
Clear	State attained by completion of the Clearing Course at an advanced org in which 'engrams' are removed during auditing.
CMO	Commodore's Messenger Organization
Comm	Communication
Comm Ev	Committee of Evidence — equivalent to a court martial
C/S	Case Supervisor
DMSMH	Hubbard's *Dianetics: the Modern Science of Mental Health*
DN	Dianetics. From Greek words *dia* (through) and *nous* (mind), though defined by the Church of Scientology as 'through the soul'.

Dynamics	The eight drives/impulses in life. *(See page 22)*
E-Meter	Electrometer — a form of lie detector
Exec Sec	Executive Secretary — in charge of three divisions of an org.
Engram	Incidents in past life which prevent a person from becoming 'Clear'.
Fair Game	Controversial doctrine promulgated by Hubbard allowing enemies to be 'lied to, cheated, destroyed'.
FBI	Federal Bureau of Investigation (US)
FDA	Food and Drug Administration (US)
Flag	The Church of Scientology's marine mission was commonly referred to as Flag. Although no Sea Org vessels are in operation today, the term Flag is still used in the Sea Org.
Flag Land Base	This base offers services which were formerly only available on the *Apollo* (flagship of the Sea Org).
FOI	Freedom of Information Act
FOLO	Flag Operations Liaison Office
GO	Guardians' Office. The administrative bureau for the Church of Scientology which handled finances, public relations, social and legal matters. It was active in defending the church, and its personnel were executives of Scientology.
Guardian	Formerly the most senior executive of Scientology. This office and the GO were abolished after its leaders were convicted of criminal offences in 1979–80.
HASI	Hubbard Association of Scientologists International
HCO	Hubbard Communications Office: in charge of the Org Board, of personnel, of inspection and of ethics. Orders are issued from this office.
HCOB	Hubbard Communications Office Bulletins. Said to be written by L. Ron Hubbard only. Usually written or printed in red on white paper.
HCO PL	Hubbard Communications Office Policy Letter. Orders or directions for Scientology policy. Written or printed in green on white paper. Formerly signed by L. Ron Hubbard.
Hubbard Dianetic Research Foundation	The first organization of Dianetics in the United States
IRS	Inland Revenue Service (US)
LRH	L. Ron Hubbard, founder of Dianetics and Scientology

MEST	The physical universe. Matter, Energy, Space and Time.
Mission	A group granted permission to deliver elementary Scientology and Dianetic services but without the Church of Scientology's status and rights.
MSH	Mary Sue Hubbard
NAMH	National Association for Mental Health (US)
N.E.D.	'New Era Dianetics': the original version of Dianetics overhauled and improved by L. Ron Hubbard in 1978.
Org	Organization. (Each org is divided into seven divisions. Each division is headed by a secretary and has three departments. A director is the head of a department.)
Org Board	The structure of the organization showing its divisions, departments, personnel and their functions, and lines of communication.
OT	Operating Thetan — advanced state of Clear
Out-Ethics	Situation in which the individual acts against the best interests or ideals of his group.
Out-Tech	Situation where Scientology is not being applied or is incorrectly applied.
Overts	Acts of omission or wrongdoing
O/W	Overts or withholds
pc	preclear (from pre-clear). Individual who hasn't yet attained the state of Clear but is being audited towards it.
PDC	Philadelphia Doctorate Course Lectures
PTS	Potential Trouble Source (someone hostile to Scientology)
Purification Rundown	Health programme devised by L. Ron Hubbard using vitamins, exercise and sauna baths.
R2–45	Release by means of being shot with a Colt .45
RPF	Rehabilitation Project Force, a form of punishment in which the offender has to do 'hard labour' such as cleaning toilets or manual labour.
Saint Hill	Location of the worldwide headquarters of Scientology at East Grinstead, Sussex. It is also the UK Advanced Org (AOSH UK). The abbreviation 'SH' also applies to any organization authorized to deliver upper-level Scientology courses: e.g. American Saint Hill Organization (ASHO), the Advanced Organization and Saint Hill in Denmark (AOSH EU) and Saint Hill Europe (SH EU).

Scientology	Defined by the Church of Scientology as 'from the Latin *scio* (knowing in the fullest sense) and Greek *logos* (study) . . . the science of knowledge'. The church's symbol is the letter 'S' threaded through two triangles.
Scientologist	Defined by the church as 'one who understands life'.
Sea Org	According to the Church of Scientology definitions this is 'a fraternal organization existing within the formalized structure of the Churches of Scientology. It consists of highly dedicated members of the church who take vows of eternal service. The Sea Org's life-style of community living is traditional to religious orders'.
Sec Check	Security Check
Somatics	Mental or physical illnesses
SP	Suppressive Person: one who suppresses those around him or seeks to damage Scientology or a Scientologist by suppressive acts.
Standard Tech	Following standard procedures
Stats	Statistics
Synergetics	One of the breakaway movements from the Church of Scientology.
Tech	Technology: the application of the precise drills and processes of Scientology.
Thetan	Spirit. Also the immortal element in an individual.
Time Track	An individual's past history which may include past lives. Auditing enables the subject to recall incidents on the Time Track.
Tone-scale	The main gradient of Scientology *(see page 23)*
Touch Assist	Touching injured or affected body areas to assist the patient in healing.
TR	Training regimens or drills
Upper Indoc TRs	Upper Indoctrination TRs, the drills that teach the CCHs (Communication, Control and Havingness).
WFMH	World Federation for Mental Health
Withold	Unspoken or withheld transgression against the moral code.

Index

(For details of illustrations consult separate list)
Throughout, the abbreviation LRH stands for L. Ron Hubbard